Charles L. Street

Witmer —

March — 1927

THE ELOQUENCE OF
CHRISTIAN EXPERIENCE

THE MACMILLAN COMPANY
NEW YORK · BOSTON · CHICAGO · DALLAS
ATLANTA · SAN FRANCISCO

MACMILLAN & CO., Limited
LONDON · BOMBAY · CALCUTTA
MELBOURNE

THE MACMILLAN CO. OF CANADA, Ltd.
TORONTO

THE ELOQUENCE OF CHRISTIAN EXPERIENCE

BY

RAYMOND CALKINS

New York
THE MACMILLAN COMPANY
1927

Printed in the United States of America by
J. J. LITTLE AND IVES COMPANY, NEW YORK

To the Memory of Four Yale Men

REVEREND JOHN MILTON WHITON
Class of 1805

JAMES MORRIS WHITON
Honorary A.M., 1856

REVEREND JAMES MORRIS WHITON, PH.D.
Class of 1853

REVEREND WOLCOTT CALKINS, D.D.
Class of 1856

"And he, being dead, yet speaketh"

PREFACE

THE material found in Chapters I, III, V, VI and VII of this book was used by the author in the George Shepard Lectures on Preaching, which he delivered at Bangor Theological Seminary in February, 1926. These lectures, together with the material found in the other chapters, were given as the Lyman Beecher Lectures at Yale in April, 1926. The whole is now put into book form in the hope that it may prove of some service to the ministry at large.

The author desires to express his indebtedness to Professor Daniel Evans, D.D., of Cambridge; to his sister, Professor Mary Whiton Calkins of Wellesley College, who made valuable suggestions; and to Mrs. Carrie Fogg Hudson, without whose invaluable stenographic service the labor of preparing these lectures in the midst of a busy parish ministry could hardly have been performed.

Cambridge, Massachusetts,
November, 1926.

INTRODUCTION

THE following letter was written by the author's grandfather, James Morris Whiton, in reply to one received from his son, then at Yale College, asking for advice about entering the Christian ministry. Although written seventy-five years ago, the letter describes with such precision the ideal Christian ministry in our modern world that it is here reproduced, in part, as a foreword to these lectures:

"Woodlands, N. H., Nov. 12, 1850.

"My dear Son:

. . . In your last letter you speak of having been thinking of the future of your life; and of seeming to hear the voice of duty calling you to be a *minister*. In regard to your future profession, I have always told you, you should be free, as far as I was concerned, to follow your own inclination and sense of duty. There is no employment more noble or worthy than that of being a true minister of Christ. But if your feelings lead you toward that calling, I pray that you may not enter thereupon without a full realization of what a minister ought to be. For it grieves me exceedingly to observe how many there be that are called ministers who are nevertheless superficial dressers of the Lord's vineyard, and who seem to think their proper vocation is in fine metaphysical reasonings, and in treating of an obscure dogmatic theology, striving to make plain what God has left in mystery, rather than, in a childlike spirit, striving to receive in faith the revelation given us of the secret things that

belong to the Lord our God, and to show the reality of
that faith in earnest effort to do his will as taught in
the Gospel of Him who came to preach good tidings
unto the meek, to bind up the broken-hearted, to heal
the sick, to proclaim liberty to the captives, and the
opening of the prison doors to them that are bound. . . .

"We upon whom these 'Ends of the earth are come'
have a great destiny to fulfil. Within a generation the
human mind has become unshackled and is fast becoming *free:* and freed, as it is, what has it not done? It
has subdued the elements to its use, plays with the light-
nings, overcomes the powers of nature, makes crooked
places straight and rough places smooth. What then in
this changed world is the office of the Christian ministry? Is it to lag behind in the race, teaching the dead
dogmas of the theology of a past age, while men run
wild in a wilderness of new discoveries and fall into a
practical atheism: or rather, keeping itself up to the line
of mental progress, is it not to shew to men that, wonderful as these things are, the Bible has foretold them all,
thus leading men while acquiring a greater knowledge
of the mysteries of God to a closer knowledge of Deity
itself?

"To see a Christian minister comprehending the wonderful movements of the human mind in these days,
seeing therein the development of God's own revelation,
alive to the woes of the oppressed and downtrodden of
our race, ever ready to help, aye, to lead in all proper
ways for their elevation to the rank of sons of God
from which they have fallen, ready wisely to combat
error in high places, or in low, penetrated with the belief
that what God hath spoken of the future redemption and
salvation of our race shall surely come to pass, and
ready to stand in the front rank, to be a pioneer and
guide to the minds of men, leading them toward truth—

to be such a minister would be a fulfilment of my highest hopes.

"But to be a minister, comfortably settled over a comfortable people, with a nice comfortable church, a comfortable salary, with no ideas of what mankind is doing save what come through some comfortably conservative religious newspaper, that is not only behind the age but behind all ages; with no charities save those doled out through a few comfortably safe societies that once a month take their 'collections by appointment,' with no thought save to get through the world with ease, without rapping the knuckles of anybody who happens to be rich or 'respectable,'—rather than see you *such* a minister, I would have you a hewer of wood or a drawer of water.

"JAMES MORRIS WHITON."

CONTENTS

CHAPTER   PAGE

I   THE CHRISTIAN EXPERIENCE AND THE QUEST
     FOR CERTAINTY   I

II   THE CHRISTIAN EXPERIENCE AND THE GROUND
     OF CERTAINTY   30

III THE CHRISTIAN EXPERIENCE AND CHRISTIAN
     KNOWLEDGE   59

IV   THE CHRISTIAN EXPERIENCE AND CHRISTIAN
     THEOLOGY   88

V   THE CHRISTIAN EXPERIENCE AND THE
     PREACHER I   120

VI   THE CHRISTIAN EXPERIENCE AND THE
     PREACHER II   149

VII THE CHRISTIAN EXPERIENCE AND THE CHRIS-
     TIAN PASTOR   173

VIII THE CULTIVATION OF THE CHRISTIAN EXPERI-
     ENCE   202

THE ELOQUENCE OF
CHRISTIAN EXPERIENCE

THE ELOQUENCE OF CHRISTIAN EXPERIENCE

CHAPTER I

THE CHRISTIAN EXPERIENCE AND THE QUEST FOR CERTAINTY

THE Pastoral Epistles of Paul, as they are called, have a peculiar and a pathetic interest. They are the words of a veteran addressed to a recruit. An old campaigner for Christ who has seen service on many fields, who has experienced to the full both the hardships and the joys of the Christian ministry, speaks loving words of exhortation and of counsel to the young man whose work lies before him. Out of the wealth of his own experience he is telling his young friend what he has learned, what he has found to be true, and he is commending these things in earnest and solemn words to Timothy, who has his life yet to live and his ministry to perform. I pause in my reading at this verse: "That good thing which was committed unto thee keep by the Holy Ghost which dwelleth in us." [1] The expression "that good thing" hardly does justice to the single Greek word ($\pi\alpha\rho\alpha\theta\acute{\eta}\kappa\eta$) of which it is the translation. The word is not used in the New Testament outside of these epistles. It means literally a sacred deposit. That translation is found in the margin of the Revised Version. It means a trust-

[1] II Tim. i. 14.

fund. Sums of money that were deposited for the use of the church were called in the ecclesiastical language of the day the trust-funds of the church: a sacred trust to be administered by the church. Such is the word which Paul uses three times over in these epistles.[2]

What is this "good thing," this sacred trust, this trust-fund which Paul exhorts his young friend to keep? It seems to be on the whole the most earnest word he has to speak, and we are prepared now to look deeply for our answer. It cannot be the details of the ministry about which these epistles have much to say. He must mean something elemental, essential, fundamental—something that underlies, conditions, controls all the rest of the activities of the Christian ministry. What *is* this precious treasure? The preceding verse suggests the answer: "Be true to the faith and love that are in Christ Jesus—that precious treasure keep by the Holy Ghost who has His home in us."

The faith and the love that are in Christ Jesus! That was the holiest thing the Apostle knew. Above every other possession he prized those great, those unspeakable riches. It is what, for want of a better word, we call the Christian experience: the experience of God in and through Jesus Christ. It is when Paul undertakes to describe what this "good thing" means to him that his language takes on its most beautiful and its most mystical coloring, and is touched with a warmth and passion which still moves the hearts of his readers. It is not I that live, he cries, but "Christ liveth in me."[3] He speaks of Christ dwelling in the heart by faith.[4] He lives over again in his own life the experiences of Christ's life. He counts all things but loss that he may win Christ.[5]

[2] I Tim. vi. 20; II Tim. i. 12; II Tim. i. 14.
[3] Gal. ii. 20.   [4] Eph. iii. 17.   [5] Phil. iii. 8.

He declares that Christ in us is the hope of our glory.[6] That sacred deposit he felt to be the sources and secret of all that he had been and said and done. It was the secret of his Christian life; it was the spring of his Christian service; it was the source of his Christian knowledge; it was the essence of his faith and message to the world. No wonder then if, when he comes to the end of his life and wishes to give to the one who is to take up his work and carry on his ministry what he feels to have been the underlying inspiration of his own ministry—little wonder if he admonishes his young friend to be sure to guard as his most precious treasure this selfsame experience. This, he says, will in the long run tell the story. It will tell the story of the man you will become; of the work that you will do; of the kind of truth that you utter. Therefore, above all else, guard and keep "the great securities of your faith intact by the aid of the Holy Spirit that dwells within us." [7]

This, then, is our subject: the Christian experience and the Christian ministry. The Christian experience of God is the one thing needful. It is the one thing that we can positively least afford to lose. The practical wisdom of men of affairs, the philosophy of our universities, the culture of our schools—these are all a necessary and important part of our equipment as ministers of Jesus Christ. No one of us can perform his ministry to the modern world without them. Yet no one of us begins to perform his ministry to the modern world with them alone. Underneath every other discipline of mind and body there must be a deep, warm, passionate experience of God in Jesus Christ. Paul well calls this a sacred deposit, a holy treasure, a priceless possession. The Christian experience of God alone answers the quest of the human soul for certainty. It alone is the un-

[6] Col. i. 27.   [7] Translation by James Moffatt, *in loco.*

shakable ground of Christian faith and of Christian knowledge. It alone gives us the key to a truly Christian theology. The possession of the Christian experience of God is the source from which all Christian preaching flows. It alone provides the temper and the equipment of a true Christian pastor. Thus the cultivation of the Christian experience should be a Christian minister's deepest exercise, its abundant possession his most serious concern. It must be the innermost secret of our life and of our ministry. Above all else we must guard this sacred treasure: the faith and the love that are in Christ Jesus.

The deepest demand of the human heart in this, as in every other age, is the demand for certainty. Amid the mysteries of the surrounding universe, the contradictions of human existence, the tragic conditions of human life apparently at the mercy of impersonal forces over which it has no control, the heart and soul of man search everywhere for some ultimate assurance upon which they may safely and securely abide. Like Noah, tossed upon a world of waters, the human spirit looks for its dove which shall bear to it the tidings that there is solid ground on which it may rest. Ancient literature is full of this longing for permanent assurance amid the tragic conditions of life:

O Life, what refuge have we fleeing thee,
Save in Death only? Infinite, in truth,
Thy sorrows are, and unendurable
As unavoidable. Doubtless there are
Some beauties and some charms in Nature's gift—
The earth, the stars, the sea, the moon, the sun,
But all the rest is only grief and fear.
And if perchance some happiness be there,[8]
There too is Némesis, who takes revenge.

[8] From Theognis, trans. by Frere.

Similarly in modern literature, Matthew Arnold has written:

> The Sea of Faith
> Was once, too, at the full, and round earth's shore
> Lay like the folds of a bright girdle furled.
> But now I only hear
> Its melancholy, long, withdrawing roar,
> Retreating, to the breath
> Of the night-wind, down the edges drear
> And naked shingles of the world.
>
> Ah, love, let us be true
> To one another! for the world, which seems
> To lie before us like a land of dreams
> So various, so beautiful, so new,
> Hath really neither joy, nor love, nor light,
> Nor certitude, nor peace, nor help for pain,
> And we are here, as on a darkling plain
> Swept with confused alarms of struggle and flight,
> Where ignorant armies clash by night.

Certain conditions in our modern world reinforce and make acute this demand for certainty. There is the vast spiritual depression which has followed in the wake of economic and industrial development and the acquisition of wealth. Many a man has discovered for himself that money can buy a book, but not the genius that wrote it; a poem, but not the inspiration that produced it; a house, but not a home; a servant or a satellite, but not a friend. He has discovered, in a word, that life does not consist in the abundance of things that a man possesses. It was one of the most successful and prosperous business geniuses of a few years past who put it on record, "There is but one thing in this world that I desire—and that is tranquillity." [9] And in increasing

[9] P. T. Barnum, quoted by Gamaliel Bradford, in *Damaged Souls*, p. 197.

numbers men are looking for a sense of spiritual assurance which lies behind and beneath all other human possessions.

Again, the rapid advance of modern science has created a universe in which thoughtful men find it increasing difficult to live without some sense of personal security. The modern man has had 'to domesticate himself in a new universe. In his earlier thinking the universe was a comparatively snug affair." [10] But the scene has changed today. Modern science has uncovered before our eyes a universe of simply abysmal vastness. With the concepts of religion one can orient himself in such a universe. But without them it becomes more or less of a nightmare. One of the best-known of modern astronomers has thus described the verdict of his science, without the religious interpretation, upon the place of human life in the universe:

> What can he tell of the origin of life? That it is apparently but one phase in a natural chemical evolution,—the inevitable development of matter and energy when the physical conditions in the environment are right. What can he say of human life in space? Trivial; a small but boisterous bit of the organic scum that for the time being coats part of the surface of one small planet which is itself a castoff fragment of a star—of a star that is now indifferently situated in a system of thousands of millions of similar stars. What can he tell of the place of life in time? Temporary; the stars evolved and revolved for aeons before the earth was born—they will doubtless continue to fulfil their destiny, to roll on quite unperturbed, long after the scum has evaporated and the terrestrial experiment is over. [11]

[10] J. T. Brierly, *Ourselves and the Universe*, p. 2.
[11] Harlow Shepley, art. "The Origin of the Earth," *Harvard Alumni Bulletin*, February 7, 1924.

Now it is not too much to say that the normal man contemplates such a conclusion not only with dismay but with disgust. He is looking around for some decent alternative to the idea that our little accidental "cast-off fragment of a star" is bearing its terrified human freight into ultimate nothingness. From this point of view a naturalistic science has been playing steadily into the hand of religion.

The personal and social results of the revolt against authority are additional influences that have made men look about them for fixed standards. Matthew Arnold once defined culture as "the well-balanced mind that works serenely under standards which have been tried and found to be true." But today we do not have standards in that sense of the term. Even the Ten Commandments are being openly called in question. "We need some new Commandments," it has lately been said, "since all the old ones are broken." A young woman recently remarked, in justification of her independence of the Ten Commandments, "Surely there must be something more in life than that." And we are having our misgivings about the social results of the lack of authority and certainty in morals. We are beginning to feel that our fathers and mothers had something that we, with all our getting, lack. They were sure of something. They could probe their experiences because they had experiences to probe. They could read books without having their faith perturbed. They had convictions, and not mere fluctuating and accommodating opinions. They dwelt deeply, and the varying winds of doctrine could not nip their souls. They may have been bigoted. Yet even their bigotries seem noble compared to "the truly singular and scant remnant of spiritual apparel with which many a man today is content to clothe his naked human soul." Moral and spiritual certainty, for all these reasons, look good to men today. They want a positive faith. They are asking themselves in all seriousness where this is to be found.

Certain milestones have been definitely passed in this quest for certainty. For one thing, we have learned that it cannot be found in the external universe, for the simple reason that the more we learn about the external universe, the less external it becomes. Materialism as a philosophy is vanishing because matter itself is vanishing. No longer can one stamp on the ground, and say with Hamlet, "O, this too, too solid earth," for the simple reason that the earth turns out not to be solid at all. We used to talk of matter in terms of molecules. Then the molecule gave way to the atom, and the atom in its turn to the electron, and we have nothing left but a kind of energy defined as radio-activity. Matter today is defined as energy in motion. The materialistic theory of the universe has literally had the ground knocked out from under it. Here, at any rate, there is no ground of certainty, neither in the heavens above or in the earth beneath.

We are driven back, then, to the inward world, to what we call consciousness or self, in our quest for certainty. But we cannot rest long there. For one thing, we have now only exchanged one science for another, the science of physics and astronomy for that of psychology. And here we are met by the fact that one of the most baffling problems in the whole realm of science is that which concerns the nature of consciousness. A sophomore at Harvard College once asked William James what he could honestly say, on scientific grounds, that he positively knew. Professor James replied, "I can honestly say that I know that at the moment I say so, I am." But even this modicum of certainty might be

challenged by the exponents of a certain type of psychology today. And there is another difficulty. We
cannot find certainty in an isolated self, because no real
meaning attaches to a self in isolation. "Nobody is anybody until he joins himself to somebody." There is felt
at once the necessity of relating oneself to another and
a permanent and ultimate self which we call the Supreme Good, the Supreme Power, in a word, God. There
are obviously grades to this experience, but I do not
believe a human being can be wholly without it. This
of course leads us to religion, if we use William James'
well-known definition of it: "Religion shall mean for
us the feelings, acts, and experiences of individual men
in their solitude so far as they apprehend themselves to
stand in relation to whatever they may consider the
Divine." [12] If certainty is to be found at all, it must be
found here. To this extent, at least, we can say that
religion in our day has come into its own. Other avenues
for the discovery of certainty have been explored, and
men have found them to be no thoroughfare. The rea-
sonableness of religion has thus been vindicated to the
satisfaction of multitudes of thinking men.

The question remains, What is the ground of certainty
in religion? It is a critical question. It is a question
which must be thought through by any man who proposes to enter the Christian ministry. However it may
be with other men, no one who has not discovered to his
entire intellectual and spiritual satisfaction what the
ground of his religious certainty is has a moral right to
attempt to speak to others about the things pertaining
to God.

The Roman Catholic Church has settled that question
to its satisfaction. We all know how it has accomplished
it. When Jesus Christ said to Peter, "On this Rock I

[12] *Varieties of Religious Experience*, Lecture II, p. 31.

will build my church," He meant the rock of the ecclesiastical organization of which Peter is supposed to have been the first head at Rome. That church is the possessor and the inviolable possessor of the Truth which it declares and offers to men. And its priests declare it and offer it in the full conviction and utter persuasion that what they declare and offer, and that alone, is the Truth.

> My brethren [said Cardinal Mercier in a recent pastoral letter] we have merely the question, Do you believe the divine authority of the Church? Do you accept what in the name of Jesus Christ she proposes to your belief? Yes or no? If yes, then she puts the Sacraments at your disposal and undertakes your safe conduct to Heaven. If no, you deliberately break the bond that united you to her. Before God and your conscience you belong to her no more.[13]

Similarly Hilaire Belloc has lately written:

> The [Roman] Catholic and the [Roman] Catholic Church are essentially characterized by Faith, while outside the [Roman] Catholic Church today, scepticism is universal. Faith is unexperienced. It is essentially an acceptation of the religion of others, which others are the Apostolic College, the conciliar decisions and all that proceeds from the authoritative wing of the Church.[14]

When once this act of faith has taken place, this acceptation has been made, the quest for certainty has come to an end. Thus Cardinal Newman could write: "From the time I became a [Roman] Catholic of course I had no further history of my religious experience to nar-

---

[13] Quoted by S. Parkes Cadman in *Christianity and the State*, pp. 342-3.
[14] Quoted in *The Congregationalist*, September 17, 1925.

rate." [15]   And Father Faber has left a similar statement:
"I cease to be an individual. I seem to fall into my own
place quietly, without disturbance, and the noiseless path
of quiet obedience offers a calm and peaceful prospect
of spiritual growth." [16]   This view of religious certainty
has the advantage of being definite, concrete, visible. It
holds an irresistible attraction for many minds. It wins
brilliant men like G. K. Chesterton, Hilaire Belloc, and
Sir Arthur Conan Doyle, who has lately written that
he "found his early inspiration in the Roman Catholic
Church, and even now, though discriminating in his allegiance, would return to it again were he 'forced to
become an orthodox Christian.'" [17]   And John Galsworthy has one of his characters say: "The [Roman]
Catholics, you know, really do get things out of their
religion. . . . They go it blind. It's the only logical
way now." [18]   The sense of spiritual certainty thus won
explains, in spite of what seem to be the vast anachronisms which its teaching presents to the intellectual as-
sumptions of our modern world, its tremendous hold upon
the people. People want certainty. Here it is. A brilliant young college friend of mine, who had left the
church of his birth for intellectual reasons, told me that
if he ever went back to the church again it would be
to the Roman Catholic Church; for, he said, "the moment you begin to reason, you are lost." That is the
actual opinion of multitudes today. Once you accept
the fundamental dogma of the Roman Church, you do
not have to reason. You are saved.

The difficulty is that many people, multitudes of peo-

[15] *Apologia Pro Vita Mea*, p. 373.
[16] Bowden, *Life and Letters*, p. 72. Quoted by F. G. Peabody in
The Church of the Spirit, p. 17.
[17] Quoted by F. W. Norwood in "The Religion of our Leading
Novelists," art. in the *Christian World Pulpit*, October, 1925.
[18] *The White Monkey*, p. 270.

ple, cannot take this attitude. They cannot agree with so pure and devout a soul as Pasteur that religion and science must remain apart from each other. Their whole lives cannot be built upon a dualism so absolute. They cannot do their thinking in every department of life except one, and that the highest, and then stop thinking. Religious certainty through revelation in an infallible church is for them no certainty at all.

The Protestant dogmatist then steps forward with his answer. Religious certainty is to be found not in an ecclesiastical system, but in an inspired Book or in an authoritative creed. Let us deal with the latter first.

Thus speaks the High Anglican who is not a Romanist. Religious certainty is provided for us in an unbroken authenticated priesthood, and in the creeds adopted by councils under the guidance and operation of the Holy Ghost, which thus contain all the truth indispensable to salvation.

I do not linger on this point, for it is seen at once to be only a variant of the Roman Catholic position. It substitutes the infallibility of councils for the infallibility of Rome, and it denies the right of private interpretation of creeds, just as Rome denies the competency of intellect to question the revelation of the Truth as enshrined in the Church.

There remains the position that religious certainty is to be found not in an ecclesiastical system, but in a dogmatic theology based upon an inerrant Book. In place of an infallible church we are offered, if not an infallible Book, at least an infallible history. The Truth, instead of being supernaturally revealed in a church, is supernaturally revealed in a written record of historical facts. It is upon these facts of history, above all on the miraculous facts connected with the earthly life of Jesus, that the edifice of religious certainty is erected. Those who hold this view may differ in the degree in which they hold the Bible to be infallible in matters of science and secular history, but they are in accord in maintaining that the history of Jesus given in the New Testament is absolutely and in all points trustworthy, that the facts given in it are adequately certified by the evidence furnished, and that this certified history is the scientific basis of Christianity. They maintain that the interpretation of these facts—the philosophy concerning them—will always be a sphere of thought more or less fluid; that it offers therefore no solid foundation for religious certainty. Since this philosophy must in its very nature be changeable and uncertain, all hope of agreement and of finality is doomed to disappointment. No man can long agree even with himself once he sets sail on this flowing stream of thought, no longer bound by an unalterable history. On this certified history alone, therefore, can religious certainty and religious agreement be based.

Here, therefore, is the substitution of a certified history for a certified church. Just as the Roman Catholic declares that apart from an authoritative church there is not faith but only opinion, this Protestant position contends that, once one moves off of an authoritative history, one embarks on a drifting tide of speculation and theory.

The difficulty confronting many minds, however, in accepting the dogma of an inerrant history is akin to the difficulty of accepting that of an inerrant church. It involves the whole science of historical criticism. It raises innumerable questions, the answers to which demand exhaustive and sometimes inconclusive examination. If this be the ground of religious certainty, for multitudes of minds trained in modern methods of thought and inquiry it is no solid ground at all.

The question therefore remains, Where else may it be

found? It is an imperative question. The Roman Catholic and the fundamentalist have an undeniable and perfectly legitimate advantage over the so-called modernist if each can claim a ground for certainty which the modernist lacks. For it is certainty which people crave. We started with that. The church has many weaknesses, but its most fatal weakness is offering people a question mark when they are looking for a period. People are getting tired of the interrogation point. A church whose teaching leads them nowhere or leaves them in the air, which lacks the note of authority, which is not founded upon deep-seated convictions of certainty—such a church does not begin to meet the religious needs of our modern world. It offers men a stone when they are looking for bread; a possibility or a probability when they crave assurance. The gravest religious problem in our modern world is the discovery of the grounds of religious certainty, apart from Roman Catholicism, on the one hand, or of unscientific dogmatism, on the other. There are those who say that it cannot be found. But it can be found, and it must be found if religion is to have any future for multitudes of thinking people today.

In the search for it I turn to the New Testament. And when I open the New Testament I am struck with the note of assurance, with the ring of conviction which sounds through it from beginning to end. I open the book of Acts and I find men in peril of their lives standing before the Sanhedrin, and saying, "We cannot but speak the things which we have seen and heard." [19] Or I see Paul standing before Agrippa and saying, "I would that not only thou but also all that hear me this day were . . . such as I am, except these bonds." [20] And when I hear men talking like that I know that they have found certainty.

[19] Acts iv. 20.   [20] Acts xxvi. 29.

Or I open the Epistles of Paul. I find him saying over and over again, *"I know."* And he says it with emphasis. Never did preacher preach with more assurance than Paul. I have catalogued the things of which Paul says "I know." I discover that they are just the things that most people say they do not know, or wish they might know. "We know that all things work together for good." [21] "I know whom I have believed." [22] "We know that we have an house not made with hands." [23] These invisible realities Paul declares he *knows*. And there is no hesitation or reservation or qualification about his conviction or his assurance.

The same is true of all the books of the New Testament. These men were simply and magnificently sure. They tell of being "grounded" in the faith; [24] of being built upon a foundation; [25] of having "a hope both sure and steadfast"; [26] of how "the foundation of God standeth sure." [27] These men, every New Testament writer without exception, are sure of something. Their whole message and outlook are grounded on certainty. Here is no hint of doubt or question. Religious teaching was never more authoritative in all history than it was from the lips of the New Testament teachers and preachers. Upon what was that certainty founded? If we can answer that question we are on the track in our quest for it.

It was not founded on the existence of an infallible church—for that church did not then exist. The churches of the New Testament, as we all know, were simple "beloved communities" of Christians. They had their elders and their teachers and their leaders, but even church organization as we understand it today did not exist.

[21] Rom. viii. 28.
[22] II Tim. i. 12.
[23] II Cor. v. 1.
[24] Col. i. 23.
[25] I Cor. iii. 11.
[26] Heb. vi. 19.
[27] II Tim. ii. 19.

And the idea of an infallible church which alone enshrines the Truth of Christ required centuries to come
to its full development and expression. The certainty
of the apostolic preachers of the New Testament had no
such basis as this.

Neither was it founded upon an authoritative creed.
For such a creed did not exist. Nor was it founded upon
an inspired and infallible Book. The New Testament of
course did not exist. The sayings of Jesus had begun to
be reduced to writing, but there was no authoritative
written Gospel in existence. The Old Testament was
freely used as foretelling or corroborating Christian truth,
but the Christian teachers had no extravagant ideas concerning its infallibility as an organ of religious knowledge. They used it freely, as Jesus did, rejecting por-
tions of it altogether and declaring that other parts of
it were of only temporary validity.

Upon what, then, was the religious certainty of the
early Christian teachers based? Fortunately there is no
room for doubt here. The answer is clear and plain.
The ground of their assurance was their experience of
God in and through the historical Jesus. This the New
Testament affirms is the unshakable and immovable reality. Here we seem to have touched bottom. These New
Testament writers had found solid ground for religious
certainty.

But now, the modern student urges, this may have
been solid ground for them, but how can it be solid
ground for us? The difficulties which confront earnest
minds at this point may be summed up in one word:
How can we be sure about Jesus? Certainty is now to
be based upon an historical fact. And is not the historical Jesus today involved in so much uncertainty that
religious certainty can never be built upon it?

I pass over with mere mention of it the modern idea

that there is no historical Jesus at all; that the whole edifice of Christianity can be traced to a myth. A well-known German scholar has written a book to prove that Jesus did not live at all. A whole literature on the subject exists, distinguished by various degrees of sanity. When I wrote to H. J. Cadbury and asked him for a concise statement of this idea about Jesus, he answered that the writers who took this point of view were not given to conciseness. However, I refer any interested in exploring these eccentricities of criticism to the early chapters of S. J. Case's book, *The Historicity of Jesus*.

Even, however, if one accept Jesus as an historical fact, there remains the question, How can we be sure of anything He said, and of anything He did? Are we not involved now in all the intricacies of New Testament criticism? If we are to believe some scholars, we have only about a score of the words of Jesus which we can be certain are authentic. If we are to believe others, the events of Jesus' life are reduced to the simplest outlines of an itinerant preacher, who met death at the hands of his own countrymen. How can religious certainty be built on so meager a foundation as this? How can we be sure about Jesus?

If we turn once more to the New Testament to seek an answer to this question, we discover that the religious certainty of its writers was not based upon this or that historical fact about Jesus, or upon this or that saying of Jesus, but solely upon the fact that in Christ men see and find God. Religious certainty for them was not based upon the sayings of Jesus. Upon examination it is found that there is but one direct quotation from the sayings of Jesus to be found in Acts and the New Testament Epistles. Singularly enough, this solitary quotation is not to be found in any one of our four Gospels! "Ye [ought to] remember the word of the Lord Jesus,

how he said, It is more blessed to give than to receive." [28]
There are indirect quotations; there are reminiscences,
there are suggestions of what Jesus said. But only once
is apostolic teaching based directly upon a saying of
Jesus, and then only when Paul was pressing for a gen-
erous collection. This fact has extraordinary significance.
It means that the religious certainty of the apostles did
not depend upon an authentic and verifiable record of
the sayings of Jesus. It was independent of them. It
was based elsewhere for them and it is based elsewhere
for us. This does not mean that these sayings of Jesus
do not have their religious importance. They have and
always will have immense religious importance. But
what this does mean is that religious certainty does not
finally repose upon them. They did not constitute the
ground of religious certainty according to Jesus Himself. If His whole Gospel were to rest on the accuracy
of His recorded sayings, why was He not at some pains
to preserve them? That a solid substratum of the teachings of Jesus is preserved in the evangelical tradition
which thus perpetuates the main outlines of His teaching, there is no reason to doubt. But the discussion concerning the authority of this or that reported saying of
Jesus in no wise affects the foundation of our religious
certainty. Thus we can keep the open mind. Thus we
are delivered from all anxiety concerning the results of
any critical inquiry into the written sources of the Christian faith. For ultimately our faith and our certainty
are not founded on this or that saying of Jesus. They
were not for the New Testament writers whose faith and
certainty were absolute. And if not for them, then also
not for us.

Neither was the religious certainty of the New Testament teachers based upon the deeds of Jesus. Not one

[28] Acts xx. 35.

of the miracles of Jesus is mentioned in all the New Testament preaching. These writers whose ground for religious certainty was so solid did not base their assurance on the fact that Jesus walked on the sea, or fed the five thousand, or raised Lazarus from the dead. Even what are sometimes called the major miracles are not once referred to. The virgin birth of Jesus is not mentioned once in the Acts, or in the Epistles. The resuscitation of the body of Jesus from the tomb is not once mentioned. The argument from silence can of course be overworked. The fact that these New Testament miracles are not mentioned by the early preachers and teachers does not mean that they were ignorant of them. Neither does it mean that they did not believe them. But it does mean that they did not need them; and it does mean that they did not use them. They possessed a full religious certainty without them. They preached a magnificent and an irresistible gospel of salvation for all mankind without even referring to them. And this fact also has extraordinary significance. It means that anyone who is basing his religious certainty upon the physical miracles of Jesus is basing it otherwise than where the New Testament itself bases it. It means that one not only can have, but that one ought to have, an absolute religious certainty entirely apart from the miracles of Jesus. It means that one can keep an open mind on the subject of the miracles without thereby having the fact of his religious certainty at all involved. Religious truth itself is neither proved by the fact that they are true nor disproved by the fact that they are not true. The New Testament writers never once thought of them in connection with their religious assurance. In a word, the religious certainty of the apostles was not grounded on any disputable fact in the earthly career of Jesus. See the importance of this. It means that one may make any reservation which he feels the most sincere historical study of Christian origins compels him to make and still have left an unshakable foundation for religious certitude.

He has left, in a word, the certainty of the New Testament teachers themselves, which was based not on the recorded sayings or deeds of Jesus, but on that experience of God which they found in Christ. In Christ God had found them. This sense of an immediate and thorough experience of God through Christ was the ground of their spiritual certainty and of their spiritual authority.

"Now," cries John, "we have *fellowship* with God." The word "fellowship" means having things in common; it implies intimacy, friendship, the reality of personal and mutual experience. And the whole spiritual foundation of the lives and witness of the apostles was that, whereas they had before known God in other ways, with the advent of Christ, out of knowledge of Him and contact with Him had come this new, fresh, and utterly convincing experience of God. This experience of God made over their characters; it transformed their lives; it lifted them above the level of every earthly ill; it sent them heralds of a new day to the uttermost parts of the earth. Jesus was the answer to their quest for certainty because in Him and through Him they had found God.

This experience of God was so self-convincing, its reality so indubitable, that religious assurance had become absolute. "That which we have seen and heard declare we unto you; . . . and truly our fellowship is with the Father and with his Son Jesus Christ.[29] When one has had this experience of God he needs no further confirmation in proof of the reality of faith. He has touched bottom. To have found God in Christ is the

[29] I John i. 1, 3.

ground and basis of a true and unshakable religious certainty.

It is here that the modern ministry will recover its note of spiritual authority. That is the great need of the hour. People, as we have seen, are hungry for certainty, they want a positive faith; and they know not where to turn. If they turn to a church that is speaking with authority, all too often they find themselves turning to a church whose fundamental ideas, upon strictly intellectual examination, they cannot accept. But if they turn to a church whose intellectual ideas are in harmony with their own, they discover that the note of certainty and of spiritual authority has vanished. The demand for assurance, for certainty, is no longer satisfied.

A solution to this problem is met, and is met only, to my thinking, by penetrating to that sure ground for religious certainty which the New Testament supplies in the Christian consciousness, in the Christian experience of God. Here is our deepest reason for keeping and guarding it. That was the deepest reason why Paul adjured Timothy to keep it. He reminded him of how many Christian teachers in his day taught ineffectively; how they gave "heed to fables and endless genealogies which minister questions rather than godly edifying which is in faith"; how others "have turned aside unto vain jangling, understanding neither what they say nor whereof they affirm." [30] How descriptive the words are of a kind of preaching today which "ministers questions," starts controversies, raises all kinds of issues, argues, debates, but does not edify or build up in a sure and godly faith. But one who has kept the precious treasure, who has guarded "the securities of his faith," has recovered the note of authority. He speaks out of an abundant and a verified experience. He can talk in terms that are in-

[30] I Tim. i. 4, 6, 7.

tellectually intelligible, terms that do not violate the
intellectual presuppositions of those who are trained in
the modern scientific conception of the universe. Yet
no Roman Catholic priest, no traditionalist, can speak
with so great a spiritual assurance and authority as he.

It is at this point that the solution of the controversy
between the traditionalist and the modernist must be
sought. There are real reasons for believing that there
would have been no controversy if the so-called modernist or liberal had heeded the advice of the Apostle, and,
with all his training in the secular disciplines, had kept
"that good thing," the Christian experience of God, the
warm, the vital, the animating principle of his ministry.
The trouble, and perhaps the whole trouble, has been
that often he has not spoken with the authority which by
right belongs to him. He has thrown off his bondage
to outward tradition, but he has not sufficiently been
gripped by the experience of God through Christ which
was the foundation of the spiritual assurance of the New
Testament preaching. Who has not witnessed the tragedy of some young theologue, intellectually trained to
the last minute, who in preaching a sermon on the
Twenty-third Psalm, takes up the major portion of his
time in explaining to a bewildered congregation how it
could not possibly have been written by the David who
caused the people of Ammon to be put "under saws
and under harrows of iron and under axes of iron and
made them pass through the brick kiln, and so did he to
all the children of Ammon;" [31] or who in preaching a
sermon from the 40th chapter of Isaiah spends his time
saying, "Hast thou not known, hast thou not heard"
that this chapter of Isaiah belongs not to the reign of
Hezekiah, but to the captivity of Babylon, or who picks
his way very gingerly among the sayings of Jesus lest

[31] II Sam. xii. 31.

he should choose for his text one that had not been doubly attested by Burkitt; or who spends much time in a sermon on the 8th of Romans in explaining the difference between the religious atmosphere of the Sermon on the Mount and the theology of Paul. Without doubt much that goes on under the name of modernism has lost touch with religious reality, has lost all knowledge of the most characteristic elements of historical Christianity, and is a pale and anæmic reflection of the glorious Gospel wherewith Christ has made men free. There can be no question about it. Our most urgent need is that men trained in modern ways of thinking shall discover and recover the lost note of spiritual authority.

The question is not, however, Has modernism done this, but is it a necessary corollary of the modern approach to the Bible and to the Christian faith that this be done? The answer which the New Testament itself returns to us is that no such necessity exists. If men trained in modern ways of thinking had at the same time preserved a warm evangelical experience of the Saviorhood of Jesus Christ in bringing God to men and in bringing men to God, we should not be embroiled in the disputes which have broken out among us. It has been the absence of this compelling spiritual power which has caused the traditionalist to attack the position of the modernist; whereas there is nothing the matter with his position at all. The only matter, when there has been any matter at all, has been with himself. The modernist should by right be the most evangelical of Christians; for he founds his faith, as the New Testament preachers founded theirs, on the evangelical experience of God in Christ. The religious world cannot be divided roughly into those who are literalists and thus evangelical, and those who are modernists and thus not evangelical. There are also literalists who are not evangelical; and there are also

modernists who are evangelical. And to affirm that all
modernists reduce Jesus to the level of our common humanity, and thus rob Him of His supernatural dignity
and power, is simply to affirm what is not true. There
is nothing in the modern approach to the Bible, to the
Person of Christ, which need lessen, but there is everything which should deepen and increase the note of the
deepest spiritual assurance and the most positive religious authority. For in the last analysis it will be found
that what the modern approach to religious truth is, and
what it does, is to bore down through all that lies on
the surface to bedrock. It does not rest until the Christian truth is founded where it never can be shaken, on
the one, the only indubitable fact, the only fact that
really matters: that in Christ God found men; that in
Christ men found God. The Christian experience of
God is the final reality. Let a man once discover that
for himself and there is no traditionalist in the land
who can speak with more commanding authority, with
freer spiritual assurance, and to greater spiritual conclusions than he.

With this experience as his own inward treasure, also,
he is able to meet the traditionalist on his own ground.
The traditionalist claims that he accepts Jesus Christ
exactly as He is represented in the four Gospels. So
does the evangelical modernist. He agrees with the author of the Hebrews that Christ is the exact image of the
substance of God's character, that He reproduces perfectly the moral character of God; but the real Christ
that he sees in the Gospel is the moral and spiritual soul
of Jesus infinitely superior to the narrative of His miraculous deeds. The traditionalist claims that for him
Christianity is based not on theory but on a series of
unalterable facts. So does the evangelical modernist.
But the unalterable facts are those which lie deeper than

spoken word and miraculous deed: the facts of souls made over by the quickening power of Christ to bring them into eternal fellowship with God. The traditionalist affirms that the Person of Christ as the Son of God is authenticated by supernatural events. So does the evangelical modernist. All real religion is supernatural. The more reality there is in any religion, the more supernatural that religion becomes. It is a profound mistake, however, to limit the use of the word supernatural to events in the physical order. The supernatural events which authenticate the truth of religion are not to be found in the realm of natural law, but in the spiritual nature of man. The supernaturalism that really authenticates religious truth is "the unalterable fact" that it is this truth which makes men free.

By all of this is not meant that the modernist ignores the importance of the historical element in the Christian faith. Always he insists, and he has good ground for insisting, that the fact of the historical Jesus and the main outlines of His life, teaching, death, and victory over death are as much a permanent part of the history of mankind, are as well attested, as well proved, as any other historical event that he can name. The historical background of the life of Jesus has been unduly minimized and disparaged. It has its importance. It always will have its importance. It is probably true that Paul knew intimately every detail connected with the earthly life of Jesus. But for him this was introduction to Jesus and no more. It was behind the history, behind the historical fact, that he found, that he came to know, the real Jesus. Historical fact as such can have no religious value or meaning. It is only as we get behind the outward facts of the life of Jesus to the inward experience of His moral and spiritual power that religious reality begins. Precisely that is what the evangelical

modernist seeks to do. He does not found his faith on
any one spoken word, on any one outward event. He
does not because such a foundation is not deep enough,
not solid enough. The only fault a true evangelical has
to find with the fundamentalist is that he is not fundamental enough. To assert that "the denial of the Virgin
Birth leads inevitably to a denial of the true Deity of
Christ" is an illustration of what I mean. If I believed
that I would feel as if I had founded the house of my
faith upon a foundation that might be moved. There
is a matter capable of historical verification. It is conceivable that documents might come to light that would
cause some revision of the evidence. And according to
the traditionalist the whole edifice of faith in the Deity
of our Lord rests upon it. The same is true of any other
single recorded event. The ground that can possibly
be shaken by historical inquiry or research is not solid
enough. The solid rock is that of Christ, who unites
men to God in a fellowship so intimate, so real, that it
authenticates and proves its undying reality. It is not
the historical fact, in short, but the spiritual truth to
which the fact witnesses which has the main religious
value. No one would claim religious value for the fact
that Jesus was born of a virgin, even if it could be historically demonstrated, were it not for the further and
the higher fact of His unique moral being of splendor
and power. The question thus arises, Is the moral fact
dependent upon the physical fact? Plainly it is not.
Even the New Testament writers do not use the physical
fact as proof of the moral fact; and many men today
believe in the one without believing in the other. For
them, Jesus is the unique and only Son of God, although
His birth was like that of other men. The matter of
supreme moment is the incomparable soul of Jesus. The
question of whether this soul became His by ordinary or

extraordinary generation is one for historical science to settle. And the truth of the incarnation of the moral life of God in Christ does not depend upon its findings. To assert, therefore, that the Deity of Jesus depends upon the historicity of the virgin birth is to assert what is not so. One surely may believe the one without believing the other.

Similarly with respect to the physical resuscitation of the body of Jesus from the tomb. The bare fact that the body of Jesus came out of the tomb after three days would have no religious meaning were it not for the further and higher fact that the soul of Jesus manifested itself as a living moral power, took command of the moral lives of men, recreated the timorous and doubting disciples into confident and convinced apostles of His life, and ever since has controlled the moral destinies of the race. The question then arises, Can one believe in the Resurrection of Christ, that His soul passed through death untouched in His essential being, that His personality survived bodily death and both claimed and received the loyal and enthusiastic devotion of His followers, without believing in the resuscitation of His physical body from the tomb? Evidently one can. Even the Apostle of the Resurrection apparently makes no use of the physical miracle, while the appearance to him of Christ Himself is the starting-point of his victorious and apostolic career. To assert, therefore, that unless we believe that the body of Jesus came out of the tomb there is no alternative but to believe that Jesus lived and died as other men, and that we have no more evidence that He lived after death than we have in the case of other good men, is again to assert what is not so. For multitudes of devout believers the resuscitation of the body of Jesus, like His virgin birth, remains in the twilight of things which can be neither proved nor disproved. The mind rests reverently upon them, but they can never be made the ground or condition of faith. But that the sinless soul of Jesus came into this world as the direct gift of God to men, and that He passed through the experience, which we call death, untouched by it in His essential being, is to these same people indubitable, and remains a cardinal doctrine in their creed. All Christians, in the sense and to the degree that they accept the New Testament and the historic interpretation of the life of Jesus, believe that He was the unique and only begotten Son of God who vanquished death and is alive forever more. Some of these hold that this belief is inseparable from belief in His birth of a virgin and in the resuscitation of His body from the tomb. Others accept the New Testament definition of Christ no less firmly than these, while disbelieving the virgin birth and the bodily resurrection; while still others, of whom I am one, accept these physical miracles while holding that they are not essential to the fullest faith in the incarnation of the life of God in Jesus Christ our Lord.

The proof that spiritual assurance and authority are not the exclusive spiritual property of the traditionalist; that the modern evangelical can and should possess them in even greater measure—the proof of all this, once more let it be said, is to be found in the New Testament itself. Never in that wonderful New Testament preaching is reliance ever placed on any single spoken word of Jesus. Never in all that commanding spiritual message is mention made of any miracle of Jesus.

The one unshakable foundation is that upon which the New Testament preaching was based: that God was in Christ reconciling the world unto Himself. To recover the accent of spiritual certainty and the commanding note of spiritual authority, it is necessary only to recover the reality of that experience of God in Christ which animated the hearts and kindled the enthusiasm of the New Testament writers and preachers. To say that this experience can be reached and realized only through faith in debatable subjects of historical writings and events is to misread the plain development of the Christian faith itself, and to deny the actual experience of thousands of the godliest souls that have ever lived. What is necessary, and all that is necessary, is a deeper evangelical experience of the Person of Christ Himself, and a more abundant baptism of the Holy Spirit. If the fundamentalist in our day would concede the secondary importance of a purely physical supernaturalism, and if the modernist in our day would recover a deeper evangelical experience of God in Christ, there might be peace and agreement in the theological world.

The religious scandal of leaving a positive proclamation of the Gospel to men who refute and deny the modern approach to spiritual truth ought to end. It ought to end here. It ought to end with you. You are the ones to prove that so-called modernism can go hand in hand with the finest and freest proclamation of spiritual truth. But there is only one way to do it.

The secret of a spiritual authority that cannot be shaken in a ministry educated in modern ways of thinking is found in the abundant possession of a profoundly Christian experience of God. Therefore, that precious treasure above all things let us keep by the Holy Spirit that dwells within us.

CHAPTER II

THE CHRISTIAN EXPERIENCE AND THE GROUND OF CERTAINTY

THE deepest moral quest of our age is the quest for certainty. No church, no ministry, can satisfy the moral and spiritual aspirations of our day which does not answer this demand for religious certainty. That demand must and can be met. It is possible to meet it while doing full justice to all that a truly scientific inquiry is telling us about the nature of the external universe, about the nature of human personality, about the contents of our Bibles and the record of the human life of Jesus. The Christian minister in our modern world has no higher duty than to discover this ultimate ground of spiritual certainty, and to deliver his message with passionate and authoritative conviction because his own personal religious life is inspired by it. That ground of certainty is discovered to be the Christian experience of God. That is the fundamental certainty. As Bradley at the close of his great treatise on *Appearance and Reality* writes: "There is nothing more real than what comes in religion. To compare facts such as these with what is given to us in outward existence, would be to trifle with the subject. The man who demands a reality more solid than that of the religious consciousness seeks he does not know what.[1] It is upon such a foundation that the New Testament grounds its immortal message of assurance. This is based upon no debatable fact of his-

[1] Bradley, *Appearance and Reality,* p. 449.

tory, no event the reality of which can be disputed or disproved, but upon the sheer inward and unshakable fact that in Christ God had found men, that in Christ once and forever man had perfect fellowship with God.

A few years ago a prominent educator predicted that the two great battlegrounds of religion in our generation would be in the realm of biology and of personal religious experience.[2] We hear much of both of these today, and we are destined to hear more. The center of interest, for the time at least, has shifted from the study of historical origins to the study of consciousness, and especially of religious consciousness. The eyes of all interested in the subject of religion, either in proving or disproving its witness, have been focused on this subject of religious experience and the extent to which its report can be verified and believed. A new literature has grown up around this discussion. Beginning with William James' classic Gifford Lectures on *The Varieties of Religious Experience*, and with the psychological studies of Starbuck and of Coe and Pratt, a whole library of books on the analysis of the religious consciousness and on the psychology of the Christian life is now available. No one is any longer believed to be competent to deal with the religious problems of our modern world who is not acquainted with this literature and with this modern approach to the religious life of the individual and of society.

Our sole concern, however, with this vast and intricate subject, is to ask the question, what has all this discussion revealed as to the solidity of the ground on which, we have come to believe, religious certainty must ultimately rest? Has it weakened the confidence which we may place in the religious consciousness as the final proof of religious reality? Or, on the contrary, has all of

[2] Quoted by Horace Emery Warner, in introduction to *The Psychology of the Christian Life*.

the investigation into the content of this religious experience confirmed us in our faith that here we reach the ultimate basis of certainty in religion?

What do we mean when we speak of "religious experience"? The term is new. The emphasis that is laid upon it is recent. Theology, as Clement C. J. Webb has well written in his little book, *A Century of Anglican Theology,* is an old term, but religious experience is a new one. To some people the term means only "such feelings and emotions as some Christian communities have taught their members to watch for in themselves and to describe for the encouragement of their brethren." [3] This popular use of the word is preserved in the well-known and well-worn phrase "to experience religion." The word "experience," however, as it is used in these lectures, means something more elemental, more universal, than this. By it is meant the contact of our whole human personality with God. It is no mere pre-occupation with inner states and moods and feelings. It is an immediate apprehension of the reality which lies beyond and behind and within all the temporary framework of this visible universe. Thus the use of the term "experience" in this discussion of religion does not differ from that in modern philosophical literature, in which the derivation of knowledge from experience is understood to mean its derivation from the perception of external objects by the senses. Philosophers and psychologists, as Webb goes on to say, may have difficulty in determining to what extent what is perceived is other than the process by which it is perceived. But they do not ordinarily doubt that there is some reality beyond the perceiving process. In the same way, by religious experience, in the deepest sense, we mean that we are im-

[3] C. C. J. Webb, *op. cit.,* p. 162.

mediately aware of a reality not ourselves, which is made
known to us in and through the actions of the soul, no
less truly than the physical world is made known to us
through our sensations and through the organic motions
which those sensations originate.[4] This is only to say
that a theology based on experience is like all other
sciences.

> It is now held by the scientists that not a single
> science is purely abstract; that all have a concrete
> basis; that even mathematics takes its rise from ex-
> perience; though once removed from it, it may and
> does go far in careering through strange worlds of
> abstractions. The various sciences have their own
> peculiar and characteristic experiences from which
> they take their rise, and which they seek to interpret.
> In like manner, religious experience has its own dis-
> tinctive character. It takes its rise from contact with
> divine reality. The religious soul has experience with
> objects of sense, in the physical world about it with
> other selves with whom it has more relations and
> more to do than with the objects of sense; with the
> values of beauty, truth and goodness: but also,
> through and beyond all these, with the ultimate
> spiritual Reality in which it feels that it lives and
> moves and has its being. The range of experience
> may extend from the atom to the Absolute, from the
> fall of a sparrow to the providence of God. It is
> experience, however, in this ultimate relation, with
> which theology, like philosophy, is primarily con-
> cerned.[5]

Experience thus understood and thus defined, it is
claimed, is the final basis of certainty in religion. It is

[4] "Concepts are the deposited sediment of intuition; intuition
produces the concepts, not the concepts intuition" (Bergson,
quoted by Le Roy in *The New Philosophy of Henri Bergson*, p.
53).
[5] From an unpublished paper, "A Christian Theology for the
Twentieth Century," by Daniel Evans, D.D.

in this sense that one may affirm that experience is the solid foundation of a truly Christian apologetic and the best basis for a philosophy of the Christian religion. It stands as a fact to be explained, and still more to be respected. The day when religious experience, thus understood, may be despised has gone forever.[6] There will emerge from the examination and criticism of the religious consciousness a rational account of faith worthy of all reverence and trust. The Christian apologist stands no longer on the slippery or shifting ground of a purely historical science. He sees no sense in sham fighting. He has done forever with the old debates about Biblical origins and authorships, about the credibility of Judges or the edibility of Jonah, as if it were on these matters that his faith were to rest. He would now fairly and frankly advance his Christian experience of God and put it at the disposal of all who will use it.[7]

Religious experience, thus understood, is evidently very different from mere emotionalism. It is of the very essence of religion that it involves a consciousness of our total selves in relation to that which is at the heart or at the basis of everything. So it is only with the whole personality that we can have the experience which we call religious. Thus the term "religious experience" is "no mere catch-word covering intellectual destitution." It is not a kind of emotional religion that lacks fiber and consistency. It is not a steeping of oneself in a luxurious feeling and a pathetic imagination which makes no call upon either will nor intellect. Rather it is the response of the whole personality—mind and feeling and will combined—to the life of God.

The distrust of the report of religious experience upon the part of men given to careful thinking and sober liv-

[6] Eric Waterhouse, *Psychology of the Christian Life*, p. 54.
[7] J. M. Thompson, art. *Hibbert Journal*, August, 1914.

ing is due to the one-sided and incomplete definition of what we mean by religious experience. Let it once be understood that the true experience of God is never a mere gushing forth of sentiment, but always a virile, purposeful intelligence, distinguished not only by intensity of feeling, but by discipline, sincerity, and strength of mind; and this distrust must vanish, and the dignity and worth of the witness of the religious experience be admitted and felt.

It will be even further admitted and felt if the Christian apologists frankly abandoned the position that the religious experience is something so original, so distinct, so unique that it cannot be examined by ordinary intellectual methods. "There are some persons who accept religious experience as something given. It is an unanalyzable datum. It is something behind which we cannot go. It is there, and that is all that there is about it." [8] One may take it or one may leave it. If you take it, you discover the realities to which it witnesses. If you do not take it, you are forever outside the Kingdom of God. This dogmatic attitude toward religious experience, however, only repeats in this sphere the attitude of the ecclesiastical or theological dogmatists in their sphere. It is, however, of the essence of the modern approach to truth and the modern attitude toward life that the dogmatic position is frankly abandoned for that of free examination and inquiry. This position must be maintained by the Christian thinker who advances the reality of the religious experience as the ultimate ground of religious certainty. He will not claim that it is exempt from investigation and research. An uncriticized experience can hardly be accepted as the final court of appeal in the matter of faith and belief. There is no reason why religious experience should be treated in a

[8] Daniel Evans, *op. cit.*

different manner from all other kinds of experience. Thought must play upon it in order to extricate its true significance— [9] in order to distinguish the true from the false, the temporary from the permanent. Knowledge of the real world is built up on a criticized and sifted experience. And it must be so with our experience of God. An infallibility cannot be claimed for it which is absent from all other kinds of experience. It is foolish for the Christian preacher to assert that this religious consciousness of God is something so apart—so reserved, as it were, for the initiated—that those without the pale cannot pretend to approach it or to examine it. Moreover, that attitude has led to all kinds of one-sidedness and extravagance. To claim that religious experience in this sense is something apart from life as a whole has often given it an unhealthy aspect. Reason, enquiry, the stern criticism of the intellect have always stood between the indubitable truth of the mystical attitude toward God and all kinds of extravagance which leads religion into a morass of fanaticism.

> As Mrs. Hermann well says in a discussion of this point, "A deintellectualized mysticism is not merely powerless to influence the world's thought; it is also spiritually depleted. As in the gospel story, the reasoning mind and the burning heart go together; and a mysticism which lacks intellectual virility will sooner or later be smitten with spiritual impotence." [10]

Moreover, the man who bases his religious certainty on experience must be prepared to defend the proposition that that experience is a trustworthy authority and that the whole mass of experience is not the product of illusion. And this, in its turn, involves a doctrine of the

[9] See W. R. Matthews, *Studies in Christian Philosophy*, pp. 6, 7.
[10] Strickland, *Psychology of Religious Experience*, pp. 271-2.

general structure of reality. It is the duty of the religious thinker and teacher and preacher of our day, therefore, to examine and to study the facts of religious experience and to know why that experience of God on which he takes his stand is the ultimate ground and guarantee of the realities of faith of which he is the mouthpiece and the messenger. The disparagement of the intellect by the advocate of the witness of the religious experience has been a serious and an unnecessary error. It has arisen in part from the unwarranted assumption that experience does not need and can get along without the intellectual method. It has arisen also from the unwarranted assumption of certain schools of philosophy that they do not need and can get along without the postulates of religion. Into this discussion we cannot go. An agreement will ultimately be found, however, only as it is admitted, on the one hand, that there is an original experience of religious reality which underlies all our theorizing about the nature of it; and, on the other hand, that this experience has from the first been guided and developed, trained and selected, ordered and established by the same methods which have guided men in every other realm of human experience. At just what point the intellect enters, just how and to what extent it operates, just what the relation and balance is between religious thought and religious feeling—these questions may be as difficult to answer in reading the history of religious experience as in the reading by each man of the development of his own religious life. But that the two are there, acting and reacting upon each other, by their mutual coöperation producing that total experience of reality which is the ultimate ground of religious certainty, there can be no question. And the frank recognition of this fact by the proponents both of the religious and of the philosophical method would go a long way toward clarifying the religious situation as it exists today in our modern world.

Approaching the subject of the religious consciousness, therefore, with a sincere intellectual desire to get at the heart of it, we discover that the central, original element in it is the sense of personal contact with and dependence upon the Divine Reality. The history of the origin of religion has yet to be written. It has, however, gone far enough to give some reason to believe that the original religious datum was a sense of fear with which the dawning intelligence of the primitive man looked out upon the unintelligible universe in which he found himself. This emotion of fear precedes the conception of religion itself. There is reason to suppose that from this elemental attitude of mind, with its welter of emotion, of terror, as the primitive man regarded the awesome nature of the universe in which he found himself, he drew his first crudely grasped notion of a power superior to himself, and from this, the idea of God. There is a universality and an inevitability about this experience which yields the impression that it is the elemental and inalienable instinct of the human heart. The early man was surrounded by forces which seemed to him very potent. Yet he was ignorant of their nature. He must have realized the insecurity of his position.[11] His state of mind has been likened to that of a man in a huge workshop surrounded by "live" wires, not knowing exactly what he might touch and what he might not touch. He sees his comrades being killed from time to time as they move to and fro. He is thus impelled by very practical reasons to make some attempt to safeguard himself. The only method is to experiment and to see if his experiment works. His

[11] See E. S. Waterhouse, *The Philosophy of the Religious Experience*, pp. 29, 30, 143 ff.

desire is to understand the mysterious power behind these forces, to come to terms with it, to know how to live with it. From this point of view the history of the religious experience is a series of experiments by which the human soul, from the most primitive and superstitious methods to the most enlightened and spiritual means, seeks communion and fellowship with the Unseen. But underneath all of these there is the unchanging idea that the superhuman order is approachable, that it can be understood and conciliated; in a word, that it is possible to establish a harmonious relationship with it. The object of worship might be wrathful or capricious, but nevertheless he could and would be gracious if only the right method of inducing his favor could be found. Under religious experience as a whole lies this great and common postulate. What is fundamental is that such relationship implies intercourse, communion with a Being who responds. This sense of communion is of the very essence of the religious experience.[12] The divine-human relationship conveys to those who seek it the conviction that God responds to human approach directly and immediately, and that fellowship exists with Him. The more religion cleared itself of magic, the more definitely it determined this conception of the human-divine relationship as one of alliance between man and the superhuman powers. Increasingly it was felt that this alliance might become permanent if man could but put himself into the right relation with the gods. Little by little man frees himself from his first crude and primitive ideas. His conception of God and of his possible relation to God develops with his mental development and the formation of deeper concepts of thought. As his interests broaden,

[12] What is called the argument for the personality of God, for example, is largely the intellectual attempt to vindicate the sense of this communion which is the possession of the religious experience.

his religious idea is given more adequate expression. The whole religious development is simply a growth in intellectual and moral meaning of man's idea of God, on the one hand, and of the nature of his communion with Him, on the other. But from the beginning his religious certainty is based upon his conviction that there is a spiritual Power behind the outward universe and that fellowship with Him is a possibility. Religion persists because it answers this inward need of which man became conscious at the beginning of his conscious life, and of which he became increasingly conscious the more he developed mentally and spiritually. We cannot account for the persistence of religion except by the fact that men felt it answered that need. It is upon this whole story, historically considered, that the argument from experience is based. The God-idea is not an invention reached at a certain stage of culture; it did not spring from some far-off prehistoric genius who thought it out by himself and handed it down to oncoming ages. Rather it is the gradual unfolding of the implications of an elemental attitude which has been reinforced and confirmed by all the growth of the mental and moral life of the race. Of course, one can deny that this story has any such significance or reaches any such conclusions. One can assert that fear made the gods and that the religious history of man is a record of his imaginations and desires and nothing more. But here the protagonist of the religious idea is on good, firm ground. Here he is joined by much of the best scholarship of our day. To deny the report of the religious consciousness that there is a Power behind this universe with whom the suffering, sinning, God-lonesome soul of man may come into communion and fellowship is to ignore the whole, uniform, unbroken record of human experience. The great collective mass of religious experience spread through all the ages and peoples is a universal fact that cannot be denied. It seems absurd to suppose that nature has produced a being who can flourish only by believing the thing fhat is not. It would certainly be a singular world if the experience, which all who have it agree is the culminating experience of life, should be merely an illusion. Some critics may reply that we do not know that the world is not as singular as that. To which one can only answer that such pessimism is an irrational as its opposite, and that its psychological origins are to be found in a scientific world-view which is now definitely abandoned.[13]

The same result is reached if we consider the religious history of the individual man. How does the normal person reach assurance of God and actually experience communion and fellowship with Him? The story usually runs something like this: One comes into a world saturated with the conception of religion. One inherits the religious experience of the ages. There is this vast presupposition that what men of all ages have found to be true is a valid and trustworthy report. From parents, teachers, the atmosphere of home and environment, influences stream in upon one to foster and to develop the God-idea. The child's religion is thus naïve and unselfconscious, simply traditional and historical and external. When the intellectual stage is reached he begins to theorize about his religion and to seek for rational grounds for his belief in God. This he usually succeeds in doing more or less to his mental satisfaction. The reasoning process confirms and strengthens his religious assurance and brings it into unity with the rest of his knowledge. It would be going too far, however, to say that as a re-

[13] This is roughly Fechner's argument as outlined in the *London Times Literary Supplement*, Nov. 12, 1925, in its review of *Science, Religion, and Reality*, edited by Joseph Needham.

sult of his reasoning he had arrived at religious certainty. This as a rule is not achieved by clear thinking; it is the result of full and deep living. In a word, just as the race has verified through its experience the fact of God and of possible fellowship with God, the individual finds that all the facts of life when put together lead him to the same result. He finds that he needs God, that without God existence loses not only its beauty but its meaning. As life goes on, with its accumulated burdens and mysteries, the sense of the need of God grows until he feels that it *must* be true. With Tennyson, he may often find it hard to believe in God, but he always finds it harder not to.

In addition, however, to this sense of the need of God, he has from time to time in his life the sense of an immediate "awareness" of God which is the final ground of his religious certainty. He knows certain moments in his life in which his soul has come into immediate contact with the Divine Life. These mystical moments are not nearly so rare as they are often supposed to be. Most religious people can point to some hours in their life when they were vividly aware of God. And mysticism in one form or another lies at the heart of all certainty in religion. Mysticism may be defined as a type of experience in which the characteristic feature is immediacy. Truth is perceived immediately and not through any labored mental process whatsoever. Thus defined, mystics are not confined to the sphere of religious thinkers. We have mystics in business, in art, and in every form of human endeavor. The results which they arrive at have not been attained by slow processes of thought; they have been given to their consciousness immediately. In philosophy mysticism has been applied to certain ways of approaching the problem of truth and knowledge. That there is an element of immediacy in all apprehension of truth every experienced thinker well knows. But the term "mysticism" applies especially in the sphere of religion; and when we use it we mean that the fact of the immediate apprehension of religious truth, rather than formal reflection or traditional logic, is the ultimate ground of religious certainty. In this sense it may be affirmed that the vast majority of religious people are mystics. They take the position that they have first-hand, immediate, and undeniable knowledge of God which is given to them directly. They believe that they are immediately in touch with the Divine Life. This, in turn, means a sense of spiritual nearness, and hence communion and fellowship. It means that the Divine Life is *felt*, and that divine resources are immediately available. Consequently these people declare that they may affirm God as a fact in their religious experience as truly as they may affirm a world of real things in the sphere of their sense-perceptions. Mysticism does not rely upon logical arguments for the existence of God; it knows God because His existence and His spiritual nearness are matters of immediate consciousness.

I think that it may be said that the degree of religious certainty which one possesses will be seen to depend upon the degree in which one possesses the mystical element in his religious experience. Without it, one may attain to a high degree of probability; one may arrive at cogent and unanswerable reasons and solid props and buttresses for the conception of religion. But certainty depends directly upon one's own immediate experience of God. No one doubts that, where we find religious assurance at its best, there we find mysticism in the sense in which we have defined it, also at its best. It is when one says with Job, "I have heard of thee by the hearing of the ear, but now mine eye seeth thee," [14] that religious cer-

[14] Job. xlii. 5.

tainty is his. One cannot open biography anywhere without discovering that this is the ultimate ground of religious certainty. Thus Catherine Mumford, in one of her incomparable letters to William Booth, writes as follows:

> I always find it best to appeal to my consciousness. I know the religion of Jesus is a reality just as I know I live and breathe and think, because my consciousness testifies it . . . my conscience says "that was real." I know it as real for it bore me up on the threshold of eternity.[15]

Similarly, A. S. M. Hutchinson, in his novel, *One Increasing Purpose,* causes his hero to speak as follows:

> In that moment of revelation that came to me . . . I had received, . . . why I suddenly had, have, my faith suddenly was, is. The knowledge of a living God, whose Presence I felt, I feel as certainly as ever since her death I have had the knowledge of the living spirit of my mother. . . . I have seen, I know the mystery of God.[16]

The ground of certainty is thus the immediate consciousness of God. And with all of us "a certain touch of mysticism" is necessary, not only to the vitality, but to the existence of religious assurance. "There are those without doubt who, if they spoke frankly of their inner life, would have to say in the words of a friend of mine, 'What religious experience I have is simply a dogged fidelity to the ideals which have grown out of my rational thinking. God is, of course, the greatest of these ideals.' That this may be the background of a life pure and true and abounding in good works no one would deny. But that there is a type of experience warmer and

[15] Harold Begbie, *Life of William Booth,* Vol. I, p. 173.
[16] Pp. 258, 261, 262.

richer than this is well known by those who have had it." [17]   The difference between this man's religious life and that of his friend who has "had it" is precisely in the sense of certainty and abiding assurance.

Into this whole field of the religious consciousness modern psychology has boldly entered.   The application of the principles of psychology to the religious experience has done much to clear up the whole subject, to free it from many vague and undesirable ideas, to sweep away many hazy, nebulous conceptions.   The application of psychological laws to such sacred subjects as conversion and personal surrender to God has seemed obnoxious and irreverent to some people.   Yet through this very process a sane and wholesome method of religious education is being developed, which constitutes one of the most hopeful elements in our entire religious outlook.   But psychology has done more than this for the cause of religion.   It has shown how difficult it is to account for the facts of the religious consciousness apart from the postulate of religion that there is a Divine Reality with which the individual is in contact.   Professor James has stated the issue in this way:

> Psychology and religion are in perfect harmony up to [the] point [where] both admit that there are forces seemingly outside of the conscious individual that bring redemption to life.   Nevertheless, psychology defining these forces as subconscious and speaking of their effect as due to incubation or cerebration implies that they do not transcend the individual personality, and herein she diverges from Christian theology which insists that they are direct supernatural operations of the Deity. [18]

[17] Strickland, *Psychology of Religious Experience*, pp. 242-3.
[18] *Varieties of Religious Experience*, p. 211.

Here is where the battle should be joined. And here the teacher of religion is joined by many a teacher of psychology. James himself rejected the assumption that the fact of conversion, for example, may be explained on purely psychological grounds.[19] And the modern psychologist who attempts to explain away all the phenomena of the religious experience by the well-known facts of adolescence, suggestion, hypnosis, epilepsy, and so on, presents a truly sorry and pathetic spectacle.[20]

The upshot of the whole argument has been well stated by Professor Pratt:

> While the psychology of religion must have a free hand, . . . nothing that it can say should prevent the religious man who wishes to be perfectly loyal to logic, and loyal to truth, from seeing in his own spiritual experience the genuine influence of the living God.[21]

This, it must be repeated, is not the conclusion of religious partisans alone. Those psychologists who assert that at the core of the religious life we find certain not unfamiliar reactive psychical processes which perfectly account for any apparently superhuman phenomena in the experience and life of the Christian are simply in a

[19] *Ibid.*, p. 247.

[20] This question is discussed by Brown in his essay on "Religion and Psychology" in the volume *Science, Religion and Reality*, edited by Joseph Needham. It can be shown that under the influence of certain drugs many people get the extraordinary feeling of deepened insight into the meaning of things. Yet all they can remember afterwards is perhaps a few lines of doggerel. The light thrown on mysticism by these experiments seems to be very slight when we remember that many of the greatest mystics were very sane people who would at all times have agreed that doggerel is doggerel. The psycho-analysts explain mysticism in terms of what they call Narcissism, which is really a regression to an extreme type of infantility. As the evidence, however, is entirely inadequate, this theory may be disregarded.

[21] *The Religious Consciousness*, p. 458.

minority. The ultimate religious affirmation which asserts that the facts of the religious consciousness, as we know them, make it difficult if not impossible not to bring God in, is the conclusion of some of the most astute psychological science of our day. All that can be said is that the God-idea explains the facts, and alone serves to explain the facts well.

Beyond this, however, the suggestion must be made that, if psychology is unable to explain away the facts of the religious consciousness, neither, of itself alone, can it hope to explain them. The point has been disputed. Professor Leuba [22] has insisted that the whole content of the mystical experience is accessible to psychology. Psychology claims the right to subject all experience to analysis. One does not need to be a soldier, he urges, to understand military life, nor a lunatic in order to understand insanity. Why, therefore, should it be expected that one should share the religious experience in order to explain it? Perhaps Leuba's own illustration will help to answer his question. If those who are not soldiers understand military life, at least no one ever thinks of going to a civilian for an explanation of it. The alienist can understand the symptoms of insanity, but can he understand the awful intensity of its impulses? Is it not essentially true that it is only the one on the inside of these and kindred experiences who can really understand them? And it is to be doubted whether any scientist, with all the acumen in the world, but with no personal knowledge of the meaning of the religious experience, is competent to explain it, to understand it, or to interpret it. One must be on the inside really to know what it means. The fact remains that "our most fruitful analyses and our most adequate interpretations come from those who, besides being well equipped to analyze,

[22] *Psychological Study of Religion*, pp. 212, 237, 239.

have themselves known in their own experience something of mystical certainty." [23]   Thus the preacher of
religion who takes his stand on the fact of experience as
the ground of religious certainty finds that much of the
best scholarship in the world today is on his side. He
has the certainty which comes from his own experience of
God. And he has the assurance that he has founded his
whole philosophy of religion on a rock that shall not be
moved.

At this point, however, a serious question awaits us.
If the ground of certainty in religion is one's experience
of God, what shall be said of that undeniably large class
of people who declare that they have no particular
religious "sense," that the mystical temperament is unknown to them, that they are not spiritually minded
people, and that hence this direct and immediate contact between themselves and God is difficult, if not
impossible?

There are two points involved here which the teacher
of religion will do well to consider carefully. He will
ask himself just what attitude lies behind this general
assertion. If it means that one who makes such a statement as this will not admit as positive knowledge anything which is not derived from our senses; that he can
know nothing save what he has seen, or heard, or touched,
tasted, or can logically deduce from these witnesses of
his senses, then the teacher of religion will do well to
admit that for such a man certainty in religion is out
of the question. This was, at least, the earlier position
of such a man as John Stuart Mill, whom Gladstone once
called the "saint of the rationalists." Because he admitted nothing as "true" that could not be verified either
by the senses or by some reasoning from sense experience, he wrote to Carlyle:

[23] Strickland, *Psychology of Religious Experience*, p. 247.

I have only what appears to you much the same thing as, or even worse than, no God at all: namely, a merely probable God. By *probable*, I mean . . . that the existence of a Creator is not to me a matter of faith or of intuition; and as a proposition to be proved by evidence, it is but a hypothesis, the proofs of which, as you, I know, agree with me, do not amount to absolute certainty. As this is my condition, in spite of the strongest wish to believe, I fear it is hopeless; the unspeakable good it would be to me to have a *faith* like yours, I mean as firm as yours, on that, to you, fundamental point, I am as strongly conscious of when life is a happiness to me as when it is, what it has been for long periods now past by, a burthen.[23]

Mill was doubtless correct. The case was hopeless for him, and it is hopeless today for a man who insists that only "proof," in the ordinary sense of that term, can lead to knowledge of God. As H. G. Wells says in his *God the Invisible King:*

Modern religion bases its knowledge of God and its account of God upon experience. It has encountered God. It does not argue about God, it relates. . . . This cardinal experience is an undoubting, immediate sense of God. It is the attainment of an absolute certainty that one is not alone in oneself. . . . It is like standing side by side with and touching some one that one loves very dearly and trusts completely.[24]

The knowledge of God so won, it must be insisted, is as indubitable, as authoritative, as the knowledge won through sense-perception and the reasoning from it. We must be willing to admit that there are windows of the

[23] *Letters of John Stuart Mill*, ed. by Hugh S. R. Elliot, Vol. I, p. 90.   [24] Pp. 20, 23.

soul through which we can look out upon the world of reality other than that which the senses furnish. The agnosticism of the man on the street, if it exists, is often due to the fact that he insists that knowledge of God can be won in one fashion only. So long as he remains in this attitude it is useless to debate with him. The best that can be done with him perhaps is to point out that by the same process alone he cannot know some of the most evident and precious things in life. We all understand the difference between things that are a-logical and things which are illogical. The finest things in life are not illogical, but they are a-logical. Personality itself cannot be "proved," and the most indubitable experiences of life are not known by the strictly demonstrative method.

In the next place, however, the teacher of religion will do well to avoid the position that there is an "organ of faith" indispensable to the possession of religious certainty. The older writers on the subject used to affirm a special mystical "sense" or faculty. They did not hesitate to compare it to a sense for music or a sense for poetry. Just so, there is an inner and spiritual faculty which one must possess in order to discern spiritual things. Psychology has done the cause of religion few higher services than to discredit this "faculty psychology" by which certain mental facts are explained by referring them to special powers of the soul. The reasons for its rejection by the psychologists need not detain us, but its importance for the cause of religion we must recognize.

So long as religious teachers talked about an "organ of faith" it was possible for some people to argue that they possessed no such organ; or, if they did, that it was in an undeveloped, embryonic form; or that, like a worn-out battery, it had run down and could not be recharged or galvinated again into action. And there was little to answer to such a plea. All that the religious teacher could do was to shake his head and deplore that the person was in so sad a case. Today, however, the situation has changed.[25] Religious experience, we have learned, like all other experience, involves not one part of the personality but the whole person. In the last analysis holiness means wholeness, and that teaching or preaching which exalts feeling of a certain sort as the sole means to religious knowledge, and discounts the place of reason and discredits the action of the will, is pernicious and dangerous.[26] Faith is the activity of the whole man. There are no special mystical short-cuts to real communion with God and complete fellowship with Him. Those who have this attitude imagine that they have reached the end of their journey when they have only begun it. Intellectual conviction and moral self-surrender, as truly as emotional feeling of any kind, are two component parts of "to believe."

This understanding of the meaning of religious experience is of immense advantage to the teacher of religion. Now he has something to say to the man who complains that he has no special spiritual faculty or spiritual sense. He reminds him that, if he is deficient in one of the departments of the religious life, he may be strong in the others. Faith, he tells him, is not merely a matter of feeling; not wholly, as Schleiermacher would have us believe, a sense of dependence. It is the response of one's total nature to the call of the Divine Life. That response is in itself an act of faith. It is an act of sheer loyalty. It is going out, as Abraham did, without knowing where we are going. Hartley Coleridge has finely put this in his sonnet entitled "Faith":

[25] See W. R. Inge, *Faith and Reason in Religion*, pp. 14-18, 21-24.
[26] See Strickland, *op. cit.*, pp. 273-4.

Think not the faith by which the just shall live
Is a dead creed, a map correct of Heaven,
Far less a feeling fond and fugitive,
A thoughtless gift, withdrawn as soon as given,
It is an affirmation and an act
Which makes eternal Truth be present fact.

Faith, in a word, is faithfulness to the highest and to the best that we know.[27]   A man stakes himself.   Choice, moral choice, is the beginning of active faith.   Certain states of mind are doubtless incompatible with faith in this sense.   The dull, the stupid, the lazy, the irreverent, the selfish, the cynical temperament are inconsistent with faith.   But these are moods from which every true man can liberate himself.   It is a tremendous discovery that the mood which is necessary to faith is not one which lies beyond, but within, the grasp of every honest man. And as he thus makes his moral choice, and stakes his life on it, and advances day by day into the moral and spiritual life to which his loyalty has introduced him, he may hope for a progressive verification in his own experience of the judgment of faith, just as when one is climbing a mountain one can see more and more of the country that lies about him.   It is in this sense that we can affirm that he who would know before he believes never comes to true knowledge.   The truths of religion must be believed in, in the sense that they must be chosen, before they can be verified.   They can be known by the experience of the whole man.   But that experience is the moral adventure of the soul which is willing to accept and to be loyal to what can be verified only by the experience which follows.

It does not follow from this that all men can have or ought to expect to have the same degree of religious cer-

[27] See Mary Whiton Calkins, *A First Book in Psychology*, pp. 244-246.

tainty. Without doubt, certain souls are so balanced, and their moral and spiritual powers so developed, that they attain the highest degree of certainty. Teachers of religion would do well to remind their hearers that the classic expressions of religious certainty which they find in the Bible, in the literature of the mystics, in the hymns of the church, may lie quite beyond their own powers. People often become discouraged because they feel that they fall far below these levels. They ought to be reminded that these are not standards by which we should measure the genuineness of our own religious convictions. They are precious documents to which we may point with pride and joy as evidence of the degree of assurance to which some men have arrived. For ourselves we may have the comfortable conviction that, while we may not attain to these heights, we can win through faithfulness and loyalty the amount of certainty which will enable us to do our work and to bear our witness; an amount, moreover, which will increase and not diminish as life goes on and as increasing evidence is given us that the Lord is indeed the rewarder of all who seek Him.

It is a wonderful thing for the religious teacher to understand that he can say to the man who urges that it is no fault of his that he cannot be "religious" because he lacks the religious faculty, that it is his fault, and that he can be "religious" if he wants to. It is true that the natural man cannot know the secret of God, but it is also true, as Paul urges, that no one need continue to be a natural man unless he wants to; he can become a supernatural man. Not only is the door of the holiest wide open, but the gate of the outer court is open also. And if a man chooses to stay outside in the cold and dark, well then, he has only himself to blame for it. If he is shut out of this knowledge, it is because he shuts himself out. If he does not enter into the secret, it is not because he cannot but because he will not. The things of the spirit may be a mystery. But the key which opens the door to them is not possessed by the few, but may be possessed by any who desire to use it.

Such, then, is the ground of our religious certainty. Such is our answer to the insistent question, Is it possible to be certain of unseen spiritual realities. Just as the sailor's wife peers out anxiously into the sea, waiting for assured tidings that her loved one is safe, so our hearts, if they are religiously awake, look out into the unknown for assurance that they are safe.[28] Nothing will satisfy that waiting woman but certainty; she is deaf to all rumors, stories, or comforting suggestions that he *may* be safe. She wants to know that he *is* safe. And nothing will satisfy the human heart but religious certainty. All other attempts to satisfy it are an insult to its spiritual condition. This certainty is not to be found in the realm of outward or purely historical fact. For this is capable of revision; this is at the mercy of investigation and research. Certainty, if such there be, must be put beyond the reach of the scientific or historical expert. It must be found, if it is to be found at all, in the soul's experience of God as the Infinite and Ultimate Reality. In the deeper regions of the soul there is born a positive assertion that God is and that only in the knowledge of Him do we come to know ourselves. This positive affirmation of our spirits is faith in the deepest sense of the word, faith in the integrity of our souls, and in their destiny. It is sheer assertion, a bold and defiant leap over the limitations imposed by the outward conditions of life. The soul proves the possibility of breaking through limitations by actually doing it. It makes the grand spiritual

[28] Karl Heim, *Glaubensgewissheit*, Leipzig, 1920.

experiment, and this results in an experience which proves the existence of the spiritual world. From the point of view of pure thought, from the point of view of the most exact science, nothing can be said against the existence of this spiritual world in which alone the soul finds its peace. But its existence, its reality, is perceived only when the soul makes its grand adventure, asserts its freedom, pushes boldly out into the Unseen, and by so doing finds, sees, knows what can be found and seen and known in no other way.

The soul's experience of God is thus the ultimate ground of religious certainty. The possibility of this experience is conceded by both philosophy and science. Modern psychological method does not and cannot explain it away. It lies within the grasp of every earnest man. And once he has grasped this, no further proof, in the strict sense of the existence of God, is needed or demanded.

It is not of course the peculiar prerogative of Christianity that it grounds the assurance of its message in the religious consciousness. All religions do the same thing. The measure of the worth, the dignity, the permanence of any religion is the degree with which it does it, and the number of people for which it is done. Mysticism, in the sense of an immediate, first-hand consciousness of God, is of the nature of all religions. It is there that they all meet and mingle. It is at this point that all men clasp hands and are brothers. Christianity must be treated objectively as a part of the general history of the religious consciousness. One cannot begin to understand the nature of Christianity unless one approaches it from this standpoint.

Neither, however, can we understand it unless we understand also that with the Bible an entirely new chapter opens in the history of man's experience of God. When we turn to the religious consciousness of the prophets we are struck at once by the existence of an experience of God so unique, so direct, so overwhelming, and so profound in its personal and social and ethical meanings that it is difficult to describe or to explain it simply as the natural unfolding of a previous or of a contemporary religious experience. Rather it gives the impression of being a breaking through of the life of God upon the souls of men. It is no longer the story merely of man's search after God. It is the record of how God found men.

If this is true of the Old Testament, it is supremely true of the New Testament. With the advent of Jesus, a new epoch begins in the history of the religious consciousness. When the angel of the Annunciation said, "They shall call His name Emmanuel, which is, being interpreted, God with us," the place of Jesus in the religious history of mankind was adequately defined. What Jesus meant for men then is what He means for men now. Jesus means a new experience of God. That experience has its roots in the past. It is connected historically with even the remotest and the feeblest effort of the human soul to break through the tragic conditions of life, and find God. It is related especially to the spiritual experience of the prophets of the old dispensation. Yet in its beauty, in its completeness, in its depth, and in its universality it bursts upon the human soul like a glad surprise. It is indeed a gospel. It is good news which shall be to all mankind.

In two directions the experience of God found in the New Testament marks an advance upon the experience of God to be found in the prophets of the old dispensation. In the first place, what had been the experience of the few now becomes the spiritual property of the rank and file. It is the democracy of the Christian experience of God which is its most distinguishing characteristic. When

John cried, "Now we have fellowship with God," he did not mean "we, the apostles," "we, the· prophets"; he meant you and I; you, the insignificant, anonymous member of the Christian community, as well as I, who was one of the twelve disciples. The Christian preacher has this immense advantage: that the experience of God, which is the basis of his own assurance, he knows may become the spiritual property of the least of God's children.

The second advance of the Christian experience of God lies in its central and cardinal doctrine of sin. The Old Testament religion differentiates itself from other religions in the emphasis which it lays upon the fact of human guilt and the means by which this was to be removed. This problem is dealt with by Plato [29] and by various Hindu thinkers. It comes to the front in the Old Testament prophets in a powerful form. Yet in the Old Testament itself no real solution of it is to be found. The New Testament experience of God is unique in this, that it both deepens the concept of sin, magnifying the reality of it and the seeming finality of it in a way and to a degree hitherto unknown in the religious history of mankind, and at the same time provides a solution of it, a release from its actual grip upon the will, and an escape from its eternal consequences. The paradox of the Christian experience of God is that at one and the same time it removes the human soul, by its emphasis upon the meaning of sin, to the greatest conceivable distance from the holiness of God and brings the soul into the most intimate fellowship with Him.

This it does by its teaching of the moral meaning of the death of Jesus in dealing with the relation of the human soul to God. The doctrine of the forgiveness of sin is central. Thus no one can understand the Christian experience of God without an adequate conception

[29] See *Republic* II. 364, 365; *Laws* X. 885.

of the meaning of the Cross.   It is the way, according to the New Testament, by which love overcomes sin.

Such, then, in a word, is the Christian experience of God.   On the one hand, it is connected with all experience of God in history, of which it is the consummation and fulfilment.   On the other hand, it so stands out by itself in the vividness of its experience of God, in its proclamation that this experience is one in which all men may share, and above all in the justice which it does to the moral elements in that experience, that it can best be described as a final and authoritative revelation by God to man of the possibilities of perfect knowledge of God, and of complete fellowship with Him.

The preacher, therefore, who grounds his religious assurance on the fact of the soul's experience of God finds that he has indeed built upon a rock.   He has founded his faith on the undeniable witness of all religious experience and also upon that particular and historical experience of God of which we have record in the Bible.   Nowhere else, it may be affirmed, can such solid grounds for religious certainty be found.   The modern preacher needs to understand this, to discover it for himself, and then out of this joyful discovery to announce his faith in such positive, real, and compelling fashion that it will satisfy the hunger of many souls who seek after God if haply they may find Him.   "O Timothy, that good thing keep, the faith and the love that are in Christ Jesus, by the Holy Ghost that dwelleth in us."

CHAPTER III

THE CHRISTIAN EXPERIENCE AND CHRISTIAN KNOWLEDGE

IF A Christian minister needs anything nowadays, he needs to be sure of what he believes, and he needs to be sure why he is sure. I think that the Apostle Paul had this in mind in giving his charge to Timothy. A careful reading of his epistle shows that he did. The young Timothy in going out to preach in that ancient world had all kinds of opposition to meet. There were the heresies of Hymenaeus and of Philetus; there were the heady or high-minded; there were those who were lovers of pleasure more than lovers of God. Into this world of intellectual scepticism and materialism he was to go with the Christian message. What is going to authenticate its truth and its reality against all comers? How is he going to turn back the attacks which come from a non-Christian learning, on the one hand, and an invincible popular incredulity, on the other? Paul's answer is that the final proof of the reality of the Christian faith will be found to lie in the Christian experience of God. Therefore, he says to Timothy, that good thing keep by the Holy Ghost which dwelleth in you.

Translate all this into modern speech, and the meaning would seem to be this. Times are as hard now as they were in Timothy's day. The duel between flesh and spirit is even keener than it was then. Profane and vain babblings are to be heard on every hand. Oppositions of science falsely so called have caused not some but many to err concerning the faith. All around us there are the

59

evidences that the Christian system, to a large number of serious-minded men, is without sufficient evidence. We are aware of a vague multitude of people, reared within the Christian tradition, but trained in modern ways of thinking, who might be willing, if called upon to stand up and say that in no reasonable or historic sense of the word can they be called Christian. The days call for prophets who not only know that the center and citadel of our common Christianity is inviolable, but who know why; who can speak to the inhabitants of Jerusalem, not only with the authority of faith but of knowledge, and say: "Fear not. Ye shall have a song, as in the night when a holy feast is kept; and gladness of heart, as when one goeth with a pipe to come into the mountain of the Lord to the Rock of Israel." This inviolable citadel is none other than the Christian experience of God. Hence the impressiveness of the meaning of the apostolic exhortation to guard and to deepen it. The armies of the aliens shall never prevail against it. And it is the only evidence which we may be sure they cannot overthrow. Take your stand anywhere else, and there remains the possibility that your position may be made untenable. Take your stand here, and you may keep it forever.

All modern scientific and secular learning has done the cause of Christianity an undoubted service in showing that positions supposed to be impregnable are not really impregnable at all. The truly Christian thinker in our day has rejoiced to see the Christian hosts thrown back from uninspired guarantees of truth to those spiritual conceptions which alone enshrine the Gospel. We discard a certified church for a certified history, but we are not allowed to rest there. We cannot repose undisturbed on the complete genuineness of the synoptic tradition. But from "Biblicism" we advance to Evangelism, an evangelism to be sure forever bound up with a book, but an evangelism which antedated, preceded, and produced the Book with which it is bound up and upon which it is based—a Book which can only be comprehended and understood as one shares the experience which produced it. It is here, in evangelism, in a personal experience of a personal salvation, that the soul at last finds rest.[1] It was there alone that the soul was expected to find rest. We have this on the authority of Jesus Himself. Is there any doubt that He pointed to Himself as the final source and guarantee of the life and truth that He came to give the world? "I am the Way and the Truth and the Life." When Simon had had his experience of Jesus, and out of the vivid realization of it cried, "Thou art the Christ, the Son of the living God," there came the answer, "Thou art Peter, and on this Rock I will build my church." And it is a Rock. It is the only Rock there is. When one has found it one needs nothing else.

> On Christ the solid Rock I stand
> All other ground is sinking sand.

To fight its findings or to curb or challenge its rights is no way, no restful way, no rightful way, to deal with so great a blessing as criticism. The way is to fix faith beyond its reach.[2] All vital religious experience is ultimately beyond the reach of a purely secular criticism. This may clarify it, may provide intellectual groundwork for it, may free it from many undesirable elements, but ultimately it can neither explain it, nor explain it away. And if this is true of religious experience as a whole, it is profoundly true of the Christian experience of God. It reposes on a solid historical basis, but it is not dependent on any debatable historical event. It has a background of actual religious teaching, but it is inde-

[1] P. T. Forsyth, *The Person and Place of Jesus Christ*, p. 171.
[2] *Ibid.*, p. 318.

pendent of any single utterance. It looks with sympathy, with interest, and with a certain sense of detachment upon the work of analysts, scholars, critics. For the secret of its assurance lies beyond them all. It lies in the soul's knowledge of God in Jesus Christ our Lord.

A modern writer [3] has divided the contending parties in our theological world today into three groups: institutionalists, fundamentalists, experimentalists. Without following too closely his own description of these groups, let us admit the rough classification. There are those in our modern world who find in the historic church the ultimate guarantee of Christian truth of which it is the custodian and the mouthpiece. Again, there are those in the modern world who profess an unwavering attachment to the statements of Christian doctrine which have come from the Christian tradition, and who maintain that the scientific basis of Christian truth is to be found in the trustworthy history given in Scripture. Both of these groups are strong and well organized, and they have on their side an intelligible and familiar moral and mental posture. But what shall we say of that large element in modern Protestantism which belongs to neither group? Shall it be said that, unable to identify themselves with either of the other groups, they are adrift and are destined to cut themselves off from the historic Christian tradition, and, as Dr. Lake does not hesitate to predict, create "a new form of organized religion which probably would not call itself Christian at all, though it would represent all that is best in the Christianity of today?"

This third group certainly suffers from definite disabilities. For one thing, it lacks a name. There are those in it who do not wish to be called liberals. The word has acquired a theological significance which simply

[3] Kirsopp Lake, *The Religion of Yesterday and Tomorrow*, pp. 60 ff.

does not describe them. Neither are they anxious to be called modernists. The word suggests that they have severed their connection with the historic Christian tradition, which is not true of them. Also they do not care to be called experimentalists. That seems to mean that they have no solid basis for their religious certainty, that their's is merely a subjective philosophy which must, of its very nature, be fluid, changeable, uncertain; so that they are, so to speak, adrift on this flowing stream of thought, on this restless, unstable sea of ceaseless experimentation. This also is far from being their state of mind. They are in full agreement with a brilliant modern Japanese thinker, Masabaru Anasaki, who has recently said that the trouble nowadays is that we have too much experimentation, and too little experience.[4] The name that perhaps best designates this third group is Evangelicals. What really binds this group together is their common acceptance of and common reliance upon the evangelical Christian experience of God through Christ, which enshrines within it the essence of the historic doctrines of the Church, and the historic institution of the Church itself.

This name suggests also what this third group needs even more than it needs a name. It suggests a program. It describes an attitude which is just as intelligible, as clearly etched as that of the institutionalist and of the fundamentalist. It is even more inclusive. It may, in fact, be called the common denominator of Christianity as a whole. There are those, for example, who do not understand the attitude of the institutionalist. They simply cannot think of Christianity in terms of an authoritative ecclesiastical system. But there is not a Catholic on earth, Roman or Anglican, as our hymn-books

[4] We may add, I think, that when there is experience, there is too little reliance upon it.

amply prove, who does not understand in his heart of hearts the meaning of the Christian experience of the love of God in Jesus Christ our Lord.

Again, there are people who do not understand, in the sense that they cannot assent to, the premises on which the fundamentalist bases his faith. But there is not a fundamentalist in the land who does not understand and respond to the underlying and central experience of God in Christ which is of the very essence of his faith. When, therefore, the evangelical takes his stand solidly on the Christian experience of God as the ground of his religious certainty and the guarantee of Christian truth, he has not only a clear-cut mental and moral program, but also the only one which is really comprehensible to all Christians. He insists that he has a ground of certainty which is not only more solid than that of his Christian brethren, but is also more inclusive, since it underlies all other interpretations of Christian truth which, as history proves, have actually been built upon it.

Farther than this the evangelical will not wish to go. It would be for the interests of peace in the theological world if the two other groups would wish to go no farther than to make their own position clear. There is no apparent reason why any one of these groups should regard it as its mission or its task to crowd out the others. Why should not the Christian church march down into history in three columns instead of one? Why assume that the single formation is the only possible Christian and ecclesiastical alignment? There are no signs as yet visible that Catholicism in any of its forms is actually dying out in the land. Again, there always have been, and there probably always will be, those who find their deepest religious satisfaction in the assurance that traditional doctrine is absolutely guaranteed by infallible Biblical history. Verily, these have their reward. All that is needed is that evangelicals shall know that they also have a clear-cut program, a solid and well-understood ground of religious assurance and of religious authority, and that they shall make it evident to others also. This they have not as yet done. But the hour has come, and now is, when that should be done and must be done. It will have been done when all evangelical Christians who do not belong to the other groups affirm their basis of religious certainty to be the historic, New Testament experience of God in Christ. A fresh realization and a fresh interpretation of the Christian experience of God is what the times call for. The hour is as critical as any in the whole history of Christianity.

What the New Testament experience of God is was briefly indicated at the close of the last lecture. There is no time, and perhaps there is no need, to expand or to expound it. It is the most familiar fact in the Christian consciousness. It is the fact of a soul conscious of its need of God, but equally conscious of its moral unworthiness which seems forever to separate it from God; a soul won to God and welcomed into fellowship with God by the Person of Christ in His life, in His death, in His resurrection and by His living and victorious spirit. Only through the Person and by the total work of Christ can men in the New Testament sense say, *"Now* are we the sons of God."

Especially it is of the essence of the Christian experience of God that an answer has been found to the problem presented by the inherent sinfulness of man and the justice of God. Thus no one can understand the Christian experience of God without an adequate conception of the meaning of the Cross. To Paul, and to all the New Testament writers, the Cross is central.[5] The Cross did something. It did something tremendous. It did some-

[5] T. R. Glover, *Paul of Tarsus,* p. 88.

thing which never had been done before. It solved the deepest moral antinomy in the religious experience of the race. That Christianity has been from the first a redemptive religion founded upon a profound idea of the meaning of the Cross cannot be denied. To regard Christ as the Founder of Christianity, not because He redeemed men from sin, but because He pointed men to a way of life of which He was the supreme example, is simply not to understand historical Christianity at all. What makes fellowship with God, the experience of God, the warm and passionate thing that it is, is precisely this overwhelming experience that in and through Christ sin has been done away, and thus for the first time fellowship with God has been made possible. It is simply impossible to understand or to explain the New Testament experience of God in any other way. New Testament writers do not agree by what method through Christ sin was abolished, thus making possible full fellowship with God; but they do agree on the fact of it. The death of Christ is represented generally in the New Testament under three aspects. Sometimes it is a ransoming from the power of sin and spiritual death ($\lambda v \tau \rho \acute{o} v$). Sometimes it is a reconciling, a bringing to an end of alienation, a breaking down of walls of division and separation which sin interposes between man and God ($\kappa a \tau a \lambda \lambda a \gamma \acute{\eta}$). Sometimes it is a sacrifice to fulfil the demands of the moral law ($\grave{\iota} \lambda a \sigma \mu \acute{o} s$). But always it is the Cross which reveals both the depth of man's moral need and the sweep and power of Divine Love. It is a "placarding" at once of the two supreme factors in a moral universe— God's love and sin-hatefulness." [6] No one can be an interpreter of the Christian experience who neglects or minimizes this central truth about it. In so far as modernism does this it is losing its hold not only upon the

[6] *Ibid.*, p. 89.

experience of God to be found in the New Testament, but upon the experience of men to be found in our modern world.

And that there has been such a neglect of the historic Christian experience, that it has been minimized and even viewed with suspicion and critical eyes by modern students, scholars, and even preachers of the New Testament, who can doubt? There is, or there has been, as we are all aware, a tendency to brush aside as a secondary and as a derived Christianity the evangelism of an apostolic experience of Christ, and to proclaim as the essence of Christianity the rather meager and the wholly ethical core of the synoptic tradition. We all know how the whole trend of contemporary opinion, within as well as without the Christian church, has been of late largely in this one direction: to define, that is, the essence of Christianity as consisting chiefly and even merely in the teaching and example of Jesus as recorded in the Synoptic Gospels, and rejecting the profounder, the more personal, and the more mystic elements of Christian experience as found in the writings of Paul and of John. These, it has been affirmed, belong to a later tradition. This is Pauline Christianity, or it is Johannine Christianity; it is the essence of the Gospel as it has been reproduced through the imagination and in response to the peculiar needs of a later age. The important thing, we are told, is to get behind all this to the words, the deeds, the simple ethical message of Jesus. The important thing is to make the Christian life to consist not in the reproduction of the spiritual experience of an apostle, but in the imitation of the words and deeds of Jesus.

We are all familiar with this plea, and we all know how welcome it has often sounded. It has seemed to rescue what has been known as the Christian experience from much of the mysteriousness in which it has been enveloped, to deliver it from those occult and unintelligible forms with which it has often been identified. It has seemed to lay the Christian appeal where it should be laid, at the threshold not of the emotions, but of the will. And it has presented men with an admirable practical discipline for the ordering of their daily lives. All this is true. And yet, viewing the situation just as we find it, the sure way to weaken and finally to destroy the appeal of Christian truth to the men of this or of any other age is to fail to exalt, to preach, to magnify, and to produce in the hearts of men, as of the very essence of Christianity, precisely that apostolic interpretation and experience of it, which is the sole ground not only of its authority over men, but even of its comprehension by them.

It is here that the issue must be joined. This is the real crux of the situation as I see it today.

> When [as Dr. Forsyth has said] we write off entirely the worldly people who care for none of these things, and the light people who trifle with them, the real strife appears to be . . . between those who accept as the heart of the gospel the evangelic experience produced by it, and those who reject this in order to proclaim as Christianity the example or the teachings or the ethics of Jesus as found in the Synoptics.[7]

And there is no need of rejecting it. Even on the strictest critical grounds there is no need of rejecting it. Neither is it necessary for a man to go into all the intricacies of New Testament criticism to convince himself of this. It ought to be enough for him to remember that the story of Jesus as we find it in the Gospels is not the original datum of Christianity. Most people imagine that

[7] P. T. Forsyth, *op. cit.*, p. 27.

when they say, "Let us get back to Christ," the Jesus of whom they read in the first three Gospels is as far as they can go. But indeed it is not. The Synoptics are not the earliest Christian thing. There is something that antedates them. What is the first thing that we actually know about Jesus? And the answer is—Paul. Paul's experience of God in Christ antedates the composition of any Gospel, and—a point often overlooked—it was only in the light and under the inspiration of that experience that the Synoptics themselves were ever written. They were written when men were in the grip of that experience. They could not have been written in any other way. The Gospels presuppose the experience which antedates them.

When, therefore, men ask for primitive Christianity, it will not do to rest in the synoptic tradition. For we can get back of that. When men ask what is the earliest thing in the New Testament, there is only one possible answer. Paul is our answer. That is what it is. At least, that is what it did, which I suppose comes to the same thing. He is the original product. And what do we find in Paul? We find the Christian experience of God. We discover that his idea of Christianity was not to imitate the faith of Jesus, but to know the fellowship of God in Christ. We find that Christ is not only reverenced but trusted. Pauline Christianity—at least criticism has made this clear for us—is primitive Christianity. "The Christian religion begins," says Wobbermin, "historically viewed, not with the self-consciousness of Jesus, but with that of the first disciples. We can carry back the line of Christian faith to them, and only through them to Jesus Himself." [8]

A New Testament scholar has recently suggested that if our Bibles were to be re-bound, and if the first three

[8] Quoted by Forsyth, *op. cit.*, p. 59.

Gospels were bound up with the Old Testament and the New Testament were to begin with Paul, everyone would see for himself that the Jesus of the Synoptics belongs to Old Testament religion and ethics, and that what is called Christianity is a new religion altogether. But Professor Fagnani would find difficulties with his Bible when he had thus re-bound it. He would raise more difficulties than he would remove. Men would find it harder to reconcile the Prophet of Nazareth with any prophet of whom we have record in the Old Testament than men today to reconcile the synoptic tradition with the later New Testament. If we must have a re-bound Bible, it would be far better to have a chronological New Testament. If such a New Testament should begin with the book of Acts and the Epistles of Paul, and should be followed by the Synoptics and end with John, people would find it easier to understand than in any other way. In a word, it is only as we understand the experience of God in Christ that we can understand the Gospels. For it was in the light of that experience that they were written. It was only so that they could have been written. They are themselves such a stupendous miracle: this delineation of a character so evidently human, yet so undeniably different from other men; who shares our human lot, yet is separated from us by a line that may be as thin as a hair, but is certainly hard as a diamond. So far from its being true that the vision of Christ the Savior had its origin in the historical Jesus, it is far truer to say, from the point of view of actual history, that the portrait of the historical Jesus had its genesis in the vision of Christ the Savior. When I say that Christ was the source of the Christian consciousness, I have not left the Jesus of history behind; I have simply discovered the Jesus behind history.

This, then, is our answer to those who assert that

primitive Christianity, which laid such emphasis upon an evangelical experience of God in Christ, whose conception of Christ was more as Savior than teacher, more as Redeemer than example, was not the religion which Jesus Himself taught or desired to bequeath to the world. It is true, of course, that the simple teachings of Jesus contain no such doctrine of man's relation to God as we find in the later New Testament. It may even be conceded, as Harnack has said, that what belongs to the Gospel as Jesus preached it is not the Son but the Father.[9]

But however it may be with the teachings of Jesus, we need to remember that what Jesus preached was but a part of the whole Gospel. Personally it would not disturb me if I could not lay my finger on a single word of Jesus' preaching which seemed to bear out the Gospel of the Son as Paul and John understood it. For what Jesus bequeathed to His disciples was more than His preaching. What He really gave was more than a doctrine. It was Himself.

If His words were the treasure, what foresight did He use to anticipate and avert that huge misrepresentation of Himself and of His doctrine which we are told began almost at once? Did He ever erect the

---

[9] Even here, however, one may go too far. As Professor Jacks has written: "His teachings, as the tradition has preserved them, are essentially the teachings of one who has come not to instruct merely or to improve, but to save, and to save from conditions which, without His intervention, were regarded as desperate. To this vision of the glorified and saving Christ, the Gospels owe their distinctive characteristics as documents of religion. Deprived of it, they lose their driving power with which Christianity originally was charged. . . . To study the Gospels apart from their spiritual context in the doctrine of salvation, or as though they were intended to make men Christians by presenting them a model of human excellence and wisdom in the person of the historical Jesus, is to study them out of their original focus" (L. P. Jacks, art. "Narratives of the Passion," *Hibbert Journal*, April, 1923).

Galilean ministry which fills the Synoptics into the
touchstone? And if He did, why did not the early
Church busy itself with His teaching? . . . Even
James, it is remarked, the nearest in tone to the
Synoptics, does not repeat their teaching, but he calls
for faith in the Lord of Glory and a life accordingly.
What ground have we for saying that if the Apostles
had been true to the intention of Jesus they would
have prolonged and expanded His teaching? Is it not
strange then that they all went wrong together? Is
it not more simple and nearer to the truth to say that
the real legacy of Jesus was not His teaching only, but
Himself, and they all together understood him? [10]
. . . The essence, then, of Christianity, is not in the
bare fact, but in the fact and its interpretation in experience. It is not in a mere historic Jesus, evidently
irresistible, but in a Christ evangelically irresistible.[11]

That is to say, even if the Gospel that Jesus preached
with His lips had not in it the experience of the apostolic
tradition, the very existence of the experience in that tradition and its preëminence—its evident and unchallenged
supremacy—are proof enough that it must have been the
still more eloquent, overwhelming, and unforgettable message of His Person, His life, His eternal Spirit. The
real Gospel that He uttered was the Gospel of Himself.
And not only for the early Christian community, but for
the real Christian community ever since, the faith of
Christ has meant not an imitation of the religion of Jesus,
but a realization of this Gospel of Himself.

By none of this is meant that the synoptic tradition
will be ignored or minimized. "We must always insist
that the Gospel lay its foundations deep and strong in
our Gospels." [12] The work of Christ has the meaning

[10] Forsyth, *op. cit.*, pp. 123-4.
[11] *Ibid.*, p. 168.
[12] A. E. Garvie, *The Christian Certainty and the Modern Perplexity*, pp. 173-174.

and worth belonging to it because it is His. In no truth-
ful way can the record of Jesus' life and ministry lose its
primary place and importance. That there has been a
tendency in certain evangelical circles to place an exclusive emphasis on the apostolic interpretation of the
synoptic story there can be no doubt. Neither can there
be much doubt that at least one reason for this is the rejection of the apostolic witness by some liberals, as a
kind of second-rate or even spurious Christianity. The
reply to this by the ultra-conservative is that "There is
no Gospel in the teaching and example of Jesus of
Nazareth." This false and dangerous antithesis between
the life and teaching of Jesus, on the one hand, and His
cross and its meaning, on the other, is against the entire
spirit and fact of the New Testament. It is a degradation of both the Cross and the teaching and example of
our Lord. But this antithesis will never be removed, as
in the interests of a pure Christianity it ought at once
to be removed, until it is recognized and admitted that
the synoptic tradition and the apostolic witness are equal
and authentic reports of an experience of God in Christ
which underlies them both.

The Christian experience of God is thus the original
datum of the Gospel. And the recovery of this experience in his own life and in his preaching of the life of
Christ is the most urgent need of the Christian minister
today.

Everywhere the trend is to exalt the ethical aspects
of the Gospel above its deeper, inner, and spiritual
truths. The teaching of the Church too often has
been carried to a position where the characteristic
experiences of the Christian life become impossible.
Contrition at the foot of the Cross, Christian faith in
an atoning Savior, Christian peace with God through
Christ—these, and other experiences which were the

very life of the Apostles, and of all apostolic spirits—
fade from the view of the ministry. After twenty
centuries of power they are minimized in the life of
the Church which . . . for the time being seeks to
substitute for the real essence of the Christian religion, a practical obedience to the ethical teaching of
Jesus.[13]

And the results of such an impoverishment of the Christian experience are everywhere apparent. They are apparent in the loss of spiritual power and authority in
many a church today; and they are apparent in a revolt
from the modernism which fails to reproduce the essential and central truth of the Christian experience of God.
If we regard Paul as the classic illustration of the
reality of the Christian experience, in the neglect of
Paul is seen the gravest danger of our modern interpretation of Christianity. I do not mean the neglect of the
Pauline interpretation of certain aspects of Christian
truth, but I do mean the neglect of Paul as an illustration of the reality and power and glory of the Christian
experience; and that is the chief worth of Paul in the
New Testament. The well-nigh exclusive ethical emphasis in much modern preaching is due to the reaction
against Paul. I cannot share in this revolt.[14] For one
who takes the Pauline point of view, Paulinism is an
open book. Everyone who seeks to get back to Christ
will find before him the guiding footsteps of Paul. No
man ever yet understood Jesus as Paul did. And the
reason is that no man ever yet understood what Jesus is
prepared to do for man as Paul did. "No man ever
equaled Paul in grasping the capacity of the crucified
and risen Jesus to help one solve the problems of death

[13] C. C. Hall, *The Universal Elements in the Christian Religion*,
pp. 140 ff.
[14] See T. R. Glover, *op. cit., passim.*

and sin, of immortality and righteousness, and, above all, the question, Is this universe run by heartless law or by love? Experience of God in and through the Person of Christ, from this central point the penetrating intellect of Paul swings with magnificent sweep around the entire ellipse of religious thinking." The man who would preach today must bring this central experience to the solution of the problem of the approach for an unclean soul to a forgiving God. If a man actually preaches the Gospel of an eternal life, his is an evangelic message. It rises above moral exhortation and sees in the historical Jesus an actual faith, a compelling revelation of God who saves from sin and death those who trust themselves in Him. In loyalty to such a Gospel lies the hope of the Church. I cannot see in ethical teaching pure and simple, whether it be in ethical culture societies or in Christian pulpits, any real hope. But I can see a magnificent future for that preaching which interprets in the speech of today this central experience of God in Christ and brings it home with conviction to the hearts of men.

Here is where the preacher will take his stand. Here is the battleground of his own choosing. Here with freedom and entire candor, in open recognition of all the light that modern learning has thrown upon the facts of human existence, upon the nature of human consciousness, upon the structure of Scripture, upon origins of Christianity, he is prepared to defend the integrity of his faith and boldly proclaim it as the only gospel of salvation to all mankind. He is now prepared to meet any attack and to answer any critic. He has founded his faith where it cannot be shaken. He is standing on ground which cannot be moved.

The modern preacher will confront, as he utters this experience of God in Christ, the same incredulity and cynicism which Paul met in his day. He will talk to some men who will question the reality of such an experience of God not only for himself but for anyone else. Thus G. Lowes Dickinson has written:

> Here is a point on which I must permit myself to speak frankly, although I hope not offensively. How many men are really aware of any such relation to Jesus Christ as the Christian religion presupposes? How many, if they told the honest truth, really hold Him to be the ideal man? It is to many, perhaps most, of the best men, to whom this whole conception of miserable sinners redeemed is simply without any meaning at all. They may admire Jesus Christ as a beautiful personality. But they can never feel him to be a Power working mysteriously in them: at most they may feel Him to be an inspiration and an example, as other men also may be. The real moral attitude of such men finds no expression in the forms of Christianity. And, once for all, if they are to have a mythology, they must go elsewhere.[15]

The real value of this contribution from the pen of Dickinson lies elsewhere than he imagines. It lies not in what it tells about Christ, but what it tells about Dickinson and the people with whom he associates. What it says is that it is quite possible to live in a Christian age and to know absolutely nothing of the reality of the Christian life; to be compassed about with a great cloud of witnesses without so much as being aware of their presence; so to have accustomed oneself to breathe the atmosphere of a pure intellectualism as not to be able to breathe at all in that atmosphere of contrition and penitence, of pardon and peace through Christ, and of spiritual union with Him in whom a multitude of what perhaps we may call the best men and women for two

[15] Art. in the *Hibbert Journal*, April, 1908.

thousand years of history have lived and moved and had their being. From the days of ancient Corinth to modern centers of culture, the Christian realities have proved to be foolishness to the illuminati and, at the same time, the bread of heaven for the multitude.

But, others ask, Is Jesus then necessary to this experience of God which is the ground of religious certainty? May not this experience be gained in other ways, wholly apart from all knowledge of the historical Jesus? Indeed, has it not been gained in other ways? We answer of course unhesitatingly in the affirmative. Who can have even the slightest acquaintance with non-Christian literatures and religions without being aware that men everywhere have been led to this experience of God apart from knowledge of the historical Jesus? All that is claimed, all that Jesus Himself claimed, all that any Christian has any right to claim is that this experience of God comes for the largest number in more direct and convincing ways through Jesus than by any other means or method known to men. It is only, that is, as the non-Christian religions—I believe this statement could be borne out by a lifetime of research—it is only as the non-Christian religions are themselves touched by the spirit of Christ that they realize their own meanings and become a mighty moral dynamic. One of the profoundest ways in which the spirit of Christ today is moving upon the minds of men is in the gradual transformation which is taking place in the non-Christian religions. In one sense they remain non-Christian. In another sense they are slowly appropriating the essence of the Christian experience of God. If, for example, the question be asked, "Is Ghandi a Christian?" the answer can hardly be a "yes" or a "no." In the technical sense of the term he remains a non-Christian. But he has been for years so familiar with the New Testament and he quotes it so freely that he has caused it to be one of the best-known books in India. He is so acquainted with the Person of Christ and has so caught His spirit that he personifies that spirit to multitudes of his fellow-countrymen. It is from this point of view of the experience of God that the Christian teacher and preacher arrives, at the same time, at the most sympathetic and hospitable attitude toward the non-Christian faiths and at the most assured and final conviction of the indispensable necessity of the knowledge of Christ if men are adequately to know God.

Again, every one of us can probably think of some people whom we know, brought up within the Christian community, yet complete strangers to the Christian religion as we know it. To say, however, that these people do not have an experience of God would be to deny the most evident fact about them. They have found, in their own way, and apparently apart from any experience that we can call distinctively Christian, the certitude and the peace which comes only by direct experience of God. With some it has been largely an intellectual process; with others, some form of mysticism wholly separate from the New Testament. But a true and valid religious experience they certainly possess. Of course, it must always be remembered that these people have lived in an environment in which Jesus for many centuries has familiarized men with the Christian thought of God. It is a fair question how far even the most advanced thinkers have been able to divest themselves of the heritage which is theirs, a none the less real because it is an unconscious spiritual possession. It may well be asked if these people could or would have won such an experience for themselves if they had not had a Christian grandmother or even a godly, if forgotten, Sunday School teacher. These ideas go deep; they abide in the hinterland of one's consciousness and enormously influence all of one's later and independent ratiocination. Apart from all this, however, experience for experience, I would be willing to match up that certitude which comes from experience born of the knowledge of the historical Jesus with that which comes in any other way. I would give more for the experience of God which I have seen in some good old-fashioned Methodist Christian than for the experience of God gained through any form of pure intellectualism or any form of theosophy of which I have ever heard. "No man cometh unto the Father but by me." Let the critics decide whether that is a word of Jesus or not. I am indifferent to their findings just because I am sure that the word is true. A man may indeed come to God in other ways. But if he comes to God as the Father of His Spirit, it is through Jesus only. It was this conviction which caused a voice out of a German University not long ago to say: "For us men of the twentieth century, it is either the God of Jesus or no God at all." And if you take the word God in the largest Christian sense of it, I hold that to be true.

Not long ago a sermon was preached by Dr. Norwood of City Temple, London, entitled "The Religion of our Leading Novelists." [16] It seems that the *Daily Express* of London had had the insight and the enterprise to set before the public the religious views of the men and women who had won its ear. All of them sent in thoughtful and reverent replies, with the possible exception of Arnold Bennett, who disposed of the whole content of Christianity "in one contemptuous paragraph." He put Christianity at the bottom of the world religions, saving only Mohammedanism—an opinion, as Dr. Norwood well remarks, which "may well cause doubts concerning his judgment—even about Mohammedanism." At the conclusion of his review of the religious opinions

[16] *Christian World Pulpit*, October 1, 1925.

of men and women like Hugh Walpole, Rebecca West, Sir Arthur Conan Doyle, and Henry Arthur Jones, Dr. Norwood writes:

> I will say this in conclusion, that I do not believe any one of these writers could keep the smallest church open for six months on the strength of their teaching. Any Salvation Army captain, any Roman Catholic priest, any Nonconformist parson is doing more to strengthen moral virtues and to inculcate faith in the Life Beyond, in a word, to change the heart of man, than they are likely to do unto the end of their careers, unless they find something more positive and compelling than they have given us in this work.

I suppose all of us have had some such a feeling as this. When we have heard learned people discourse upon spiritual realities, entirely apart from the Christian experience, we have felt that a child truly and honestly instructed in the Christian faith actually knows more and knows better about God, prayer, faith, immortality—religion in a word—than these men and women with all their acumen and secular learning. There is a warmth, a color, a vividness, a robustness about the Christian experience which cannot be won in any other way. "Thou hast hid these things from the wise and prudent, and has revealed them unto babes." [17]

Other thoughtful minds are carefully scrutinizing the content of the Christian experience and are asking themselves to what extent it can be held to be the final authority in religion.

> It is the habit nowadays to assume that, whatever else may be open to criticism, one thing stands clear and firm and unchanging: the typical Christian ex-

[17] Luke x. 21.

perience,—that personal experience of Christ which
it is supposed that only Christians may fairly expect
to have. Christian experience is indeed placed on the
pedestal from which the Church and the Bible have
in succession been cast down. It is coming to be
regarded as an infallible authority. It is surely clear
that we need to criticize the new apologetic. Questions are being asked about it that need to be answered: How far is the modern Christian experience
continuous with the ancient, so that we can claim for
it a more than temporary validity? How far does it
spring from the real person of Christ, or how far has
it been derived from things that we have been taught
to think about Him? What proportion of Christians
have this experience in the center of their religious
faith? Can an experience of any kind be evidence of
anything beyond itself? In what way can it validate,
if at all, the historical statement and dogmatic beliefs
of Christianity? Can any experience, anything on
the mystical side of man, be regarded as that which
matters most in religion? [18]

Here are questions which we are glad to face. Here
is where we welcome debate. And upon closest historical and psychological scrutiny we are ready to defend the
traditional experience of God in Christ as the ground of
religious certainty. For lack of time we take only the
first question and the last: How far is the modern consciousness of Christ continuous with the ancient, so that
we can claim for it more than temporary validity? I
suppose that there is one sure way of answering that
question. This experience will utter itself in the language
of devotion. Has this language remained the same, or
has it changed with the ages? Is it identical today with
what it was centuries ago? I take up my hymn-book. I

[18] J. A. Thomson, art. "Post-Modernism," *Hibbert Journal*,
July, 1914.

imagine people unfamiliar with the dates of hymns.   I
give them two of these hymns:

> Shepherd of tender youth
> Guiding in love and truth
> Through devious ways,

and again

> Saviour like a shepherd lead us,
> Much we need thy tender care.

Here is identical experience of Christ as the present shepherd and guide of men. One is ancient and one is modern. One is the earliest Christian hymn, dating from
about 200 A. D. The other was written in the nineteenth
century. But the experience is the same. Or I take two
other hymns:

> Jesus, the very thought of thee
> With sweetness fills my breast.

and

> Jesus, these eyes have never seen
> That radiant form of Thine.

Again, the consciousness of Christ as indwelling presence
is expressed in almost identical language in the two
hymns. But the one was written by St. Bernard of Clair-
vaux in the eleventh century; the other by a Congre-
gational minister of Connecticut in the nineteenth. One
may explore diaries of spiritual experience, records of
confessions, and find intimate cumulative proof that the
modern experience of Christ is identical with the ancient
and that it has permanent validity. The experience of
Christ Himself is the same yesterday, today, and forever.

Or take the last question: Can any experience, anything on the mystical side of man, be regarded as that
which matters most in religion? Well, what does matter
most in religion? I suppose that Christians of all schools

could agree at least on the answer to this question. What
matters most in religion is the man whom religion produces. Character is the final proof of religious truth.
"The final mark of truth is not intellectual consistency,
but that the thing accepted as true thereupon brings to
the man who accepts it power, motive, and a state of
personal honour as he thinks about God." It is to this test
that we willingly subject the experience of God in Christ.
It is the sheer moral and personal results of it that indi-
cate its reality. Here is no mere form of occultism, no
mere private initiation into divine mysteries, no form of
ecstasy or rapture apart from the sheerest heroism in
daily life. Here is the most practical lever which has
ever been discovered to make a bad man good, a good
man better. It is by the fruits of this experience that we
know its truth. The Christian character is the proof of
the truth of this Christian experience.[19] Character is the
final thing. Manhood is the supreme reality. And judged
by its power to produce character, to create men, we can
confidently affirm that the Christian experience is "that
which matters most in religion." "But as many as received Him, to them gave He power to become the sons
of God." [20] There is the test of the validity of the
Christian experience. You never knew and I never knew
a finer human being than one who had found through
Christ his experience of God. From the point of view
of power, Harnack once said, "There is no such thing as
comparative religion." You may compare religion in
other ways, but when it comes to sheer moral power the
supremacy of the Christian experience of God is such

[19] "If the fruits for life of the state of conversion are good, we
ought to idealize it and venerate it even though it be a piece of
natural psychology; if not, we ought to make short work of it,
no matter what supernatural Being may have infused it" (William James, *Varieties of Religious Experience*, p. 237).
[20] John i, 12.

that comparison comes to an end. Professor Seelye has said that he knew of no man in antiquity to whom could properly be given the name "holy." But how many holy men and women has the experience of God in Christ produced? If character is what "matters most in religion," and if the Christian experience creates the highest that we know in character, what further authentication does it need? When or where do we expect to see or want to see better men and women than the saints of our own hearthstones and firesides, who have worn neither halo, girdle, or sandals, but whose lives have shown a more than earthly beauty? Ask them the secret of their living, and their answer is "The life that I live, I live by the faith of the Son of God who loved me and gave Himself for me." Match character for character. Take the noblest life you know, or of which you have ever read, which has been untouched by the Christian inspiration, and stand it beside any one of a multitude of humble men and women whose Christian experience of God has been the secret of their living. Does not comparison really cease? Here is a certain character and disposition of which you cannot tell whence it cometh nor whither it goeth. There seems to be a certain divine atmosphere about it and an afflatus that is eternal. Where did he get it? from society? from those around him? by the inoculation of crowds and masses? They all answer, "It is not found in us." It is not a reflection of the world that is without; rather it rises up from some fount that is within. We know not whence it cometh. It has God's breath upon it. You are never prepared for what it will do next. It seems to move from a far-off center, and in spite of its transparency and sweetness it fills you with awe. It is the life that is hid with Christ in God. Ask him the source of his power, and he will say, "It is not I that live, but Christ that liveth in me."

When, in a word, one asks what it does, one comes to the conclusion that this experience of God in Christ is indeed "what matters most in religion."

I admit that this experience may be easier for some than for others. I admit that it may go farther and deeper for some than for others. But to the extent and to the degree that it may provide solid ground for religious certainty, I believe it to be within the reach of all. It demands for its attainment, however, a high degree of moral courage. All religious experience is at bottom, *au fond,* an adventure of the soul; in its essence, it is "an experiment that ends in experience"; it is the loyal advance of the whole personality into the realm of the unknown, which becomes known only as one is ready and willing to advance without knowing. Similarly, the distinctively Christian experience is won, not by any strange raptures and outpourings, not by visions and ecstasies, but by the humble submission of the soul to the tutelage, the guidance, the influence of Jesus. The Christian experience, in a word, lies at the threshold of a courageous and a consecrated will. We have made too much of the element of feeling in the Christian experience. At least we have made a mistake in isolating it. The Christian experience is the result and the reward of Christian discipleship. It ought never to be made the condition of it. By discipleship is meant just what Jesus meant by it, a willingness to take up one's cross and follow Him. But, as the whole record alike of New Testament history and of Christian biography shows, to follow Him is inevitably to be led into fellowship with God. In addition to moral courage, however, there is needed one of the most difficult and the most neglected of all the virtues, the virtue of humility. A personal humility would go far in the direction of solving the spiritual quandaries and doubts of many a modern mind. It is only as we become as little children that we shall enter into this Kingdom. If we look into the lives of the best people we have known, we will find that it is thus that they have entered into it. The most peculiar thing about them is "the child's heart they bear within the man's." [21] It is the absence of a childlike humility which bars many from entering into the realities of the Christian experience. If they could be persuaded to put off their intellectual hardness and their critical apparatus, and as simple, contrite-hearted children of God seek to know Him, they would themselves be surprised at the fresh revelations of His love and life that await them.

The Christian minister should seek always to lead men into this experience of God in Christ. He should remember that not until the Jesus of history has become the Christ of experience has the believer begun to realize in his own life the Christianity of the New Testament, or to possess the ultimate guarantees of religious certainty. He may begin his Christian discipleship by seeking to follow Jesus, to obey His commandments, to imitate His example, and to do His will. But Christian people ought to be taught that the promise of Christ, the testimony of the New Testament, and the witness of all saintly souls amply prove that a higher and a deeper experience of His Person awaits them, into which, if they will, they may press.

If the Christian experience of God is thus within the reach of every disciple of Christ, it must be the possession in abundant measure of every man who aspires to be His apostle, His messenger. It is in proportion as we possess this good thing that our ministry will be effective, that our message will have carrying power, that the gospel we preach will find entrance into the hearts of men and into the life of the world. It is the possession of this

[21] See J. C. Shairp, *Culture and Religion*, p. 130.

experience which guarantees the proclamation of a positive faith. It was because the lives of the early Apostles were literally flooded with the inpouring of this experience that "they went everywhere preaching the word." [22] You cannot find a discouraged or a minor note in all the New Testament preaching. Those early preachers confronted apparently insuperable obstacles in the joyful confidence of their new-found experience of God. The recovery of that confidence, of that magnificent assurance, is the most urgent need of the Christian ministry in our modern world. And for the recovery of that confidence we need also the rediscovery of the experience which underlay and produced it. Wherever you find a preacher who speaks with spiritual authority, you find one who knows the meaning of this experience. And how welcome and refreshing his message is! Where other men pause, he does not hesitate. Where other men are doubtful, he is confident. Where other men raise questions, he answers them. Where others sound no positive note, his trumpet gives forth no uncertain sound. It is the minister of God who has kept "that good thing," the faith and the love that are in Christ Jesus, who himself has known this "felt salvation" (if I may borrow a phrase from Dr. Forsyth), who can deliver those to whom he is sent of God to minister from every last harassing doubt, from every corroding fear, and lead them to a peace that passeth knowledge, to a light that knows no darkness, to a life that never ends.

[22] Acts viii. 4.

CHAPTER IV

THE CHRISTIAN EXPERIENCE AND CHRISTIAN THEOLOGY

CHRISTIAN theology may be defined as the effort to describe in intelligible terms the report of the Christian experience. There would be no theology if there were no experience. Experience comes first. The effort to define and to explain that experience comes next. But of course it comes. Man cannot remain a thinking and a reasoning being without at least making the effort to explain in rational terms what he has felt and experienced. From this point of view alone we perceive at once how idle it is to decry the science of theology. The word theology simply means speaking or thinking about God. When men try to tell what God means to them, that is their theology. Perhaps laymen and ministers alike would be a little more interested in theology if they had a little more religion. Can a man have a real experience of any kind and not try to describe it? If, then, he describes nothing, is it not that he has little to describe? Paul had something to describe, and his description of it is spread all over the New Testament. Augustine and Luther and Wesley had something to describe, and their descriptions of it are among the permanent monuments of human thought. And if men today in the pulpit and out of it had something vital and meaningful to describe, they could not help trying to describe it. The absence of a theology can only mean the poverty of experience.

Few ideas will prove more serviceable to the Christian minister than the steady remembrance that experience comes before theology. If the churches of the nine-teenth century had remembered this they would never have committed the tragic blunder of making theology instead of experience a test of Christian discipleship. Multitudes of godly men and women, of whom Abraham Lincoln was one, were prevented from becoming church members because of the wholly unscriptural practice of testing their fitness by the correctness of their theological opinions. That day has gone, or it is fast going. The Christian minister today has no more important task than to distinguish carefully between the possession of a Chris-tian experience and the ability to describe and to ex-plain that experience. What he should look for is the presence of some experience of God and of Jesus Christ. It is this which qualifies for discipleship, however little one may be able to define that experience.

No method will be found more fruitful in dealing with the intellectual difficulties in which many thoughtful people find themselves involved than that of drawing the same careful line between possessing experience and ex-plaining it. When this is done, it will usually be found that the doubt concerns not the fact, but some explana-tion of the fact; not the experience, but some definition of it. One does not really doubt God, but he doubts some childish, some ancient, some medieval conception of God; or he doubts because of his inability to frame any ade-quate or satisfying definition or conception of God. But the moment that the mind is shifted from the difficulties involved in describing one's experience of God to the fact of that experience; the moment the question is asked, "Have you never felt the reality of God in your life? Have you never had the experience of feeling that He in a real sense has come to your aid, or that He has claimed your allegiance?" you discover in most cases that this experience of God is admitted and acknowledged. The difficulties are not with the experience, but with the attempt to describe it in terms that are intellectually satisfying.   Similarly in the case of the Person of Christ. When people say that they doubt Christ, or that they doubt the divinity of Christ, in the vast majority of cases it is not Christ Himself whom they doubt, but the various attempts which have been made to explain His Person in intelligible thought-forms.   It is of these thought-forms that they are thinking, not of the Person who is behind them.   If, then, the attention is withdrawn from the intellectual terms and directed to Christ Himself, there is almost always an instant and instinctive recognition of the uniqueness, the moral apartness of Christ.   This is a matter of intuition.   It cannot be questioned; much less can it be denied.   The difficulty lies not in the instinctive recognition of the essential divinity of Christ, but in the intellectual attempts which have been made to describe or to define Him.   Thus one finds solid standing ground on the indubitable fact of one's experience of God and of Christ.   The duty of attempting to define that experience will always remain.   But our inability to do this to our own intellectual satisfaction can never invalidate the fact of the experience which underlies our thinking, which constitutes our right to call ourselves Christians.   Always one can distinguish between the fact of the experience and the intellectual explanation of that experience.   Just as one can know the beauty of a rose without possessing a knowledge of botany; just as one can see the loveliness of a rainbow without understanding the laws of the spectrum, so one can possess the reality of the Christian experience without knowing much of the theology which explains and describes it.   It is not necessary to be a theologian in order to be a Christian.

But, if one be a Christian, he will always want, in a way, to be a theologian.   That is, he will continually busy his mind with the report of his Christian experience and try to define it as best he may. Because religion comes first, it does not follow that theology does not come at all; because we do not need to define a faith in order to have a faith, it does not follow that having a faith we ought not to seek to define it. What we call Christian theology, therefore, is simply the story of the various attempts which have been made to describe in intelligible terms the content of the Christian experience. The experience has remained essentially the same. But the description of it has varied from age to age. Men always describe their experiences in terms which are familiar to them. They draw their illustrations from the world as they understand it, and their ideas are determined by contemporary science and morals. These ideas change as men's conception of the world changes and as their moral standards advance. Thus the Christian experience of God is permanent, but the descriptions of that experience are, of necessity, temporary.

The failure to grasp this simple distinction has done much damage to the cause of religion. Many conservative theologians have made the mistake of insisting not only that the Christian experience must be preserved unaltered and unalterable, which is indeed true, but that some historic description of it must also be maintained: in other words, that the experience cannot be reproduced unless it is described in the same terms in which it was described centuries ago. This manifestly is not true. What the popular impatience with theology often signifies is resistance to the attempt to identify the Incarnation with a philosophy of it, the Atonement with the governmental theory of it, the process of the spiritual life with some medieval interpretation of it. It is not true to say that one must believe in the Atonement as Calvin did or not believe in it at all. That dilemma simply does not exist. One cannot identify the Christian experience with any historic attempt to explain that experience.[1] The conservative theologian in our day is right in insisting that, if we are to remain Christians in the historic sense of that term, we must preserve the essential elements of the historic Christian experience. He is wrong in insisting that the only way to do this is to preserve also some description of that experience in thought-forms which have become antiquated and outworn. The so-called modernist is right in resisting the tyranny of the old statements of truth, but he is often wrong in failing to recognize that these are but antiquated expressions of a deep and permanently valid experience. For the student of theology these old dogmas thus have a deep and permanent interest. He neither accepts them as final statements of truth, nor rejects them as outworn formulas which have lost all interest and importance. The presupposition upon which he proceeds is that these dogmatic survivals are almost sure to be the more or less imperfect utterance of some precious experience. Even the most terrible of the old Calvinistic doctrines are still grand when one contemplates "the moral idealism, the high ethical disinterestedness for which [they] stand."

In disowning the form, it would be an unspeakable loss to miss the spirit. We must break through the form of the doctrine into the life of which it is often but a sorrowful memorial. Under the systematic exhibition of the decrees of God, under election, atonement, regeneration, justification, sanctification, under heaven and hell and the whole edifice of traditional theology there is a vital meaning which we cannot afford to miss.[2]

[1] One cannot test the reality of the experience by the use of a formula. On the contrary, the test of every theological formula is this: does it or does it not accord with Christian experience?
[2] G. A. Gordon, *Ultimate Conceptions of Faith*, pp. 95, 96.

It is the high duty of one who would present to our modern world a theology which is adequate for human needs to discover the immense moral meanings underneath these old theological categories which describe—in antiquated form, it may be,—some of the permanent realities of the Christian experience of God. The modern teacher of religion, equipped with all the apparatus of the secular disciplines, needs to be steeped in the message of these old historic formulas. He will not crowd them down on the modern mind, but he will brood over them until they are made to yield the precious and living truth which they contain, to the immense enriching of his mind and of his teaching. A modern and so-called liberal ministry needs a deep reverence for the ancient and historic doctrines, provoking thought, challenging interpretation, and so enlarging and enriching the mind of the interpreter. Thus he will take no interest in the phrases "old theology" and "new theology." There is but one Truth for him, the Christian experience of God, expressing itself from age to age in different terms with different accent, but with identity of spirit. If the so-called modernist would give good evidence that he possesses the spirit, there is good ground for believing that the conservative would be less insistent that he should accept the form. There is opened up here the suggestion of a possible peace in our theological world.

Besides holding to the essential elements of the Christian experience, however, there is great need in our day that men should endeavor to describe it in terms that are suited to the thought-forms of our modern world. Too often the position is taken that, so long as one possesses the experience, no necessity exists for attempting to describe it. Yet the failure to do so can have but one result. It will mean eventually that even the experience that we do have will grow vague, unsatisfying, unreal.

This, then, is the task that is laid upon us, the description in terms that men can understand of the one, unchanged, and unchanging experience of God in Christ. To supply an interpretation of the total Christian consciousness as it has come down to us through Christ and His apostles, through the Church and through councils, through medieval monk and scholar, through puritan and reformer, in the language that men speak today—this is our duty. To present in terms of reason an account of all this precious experience—this is our calling. We must approach our task in our own way. The old idea was that there were certain pronouncements of doctrine that whosoever would be saved must believe. These statements had come down from inspired sources and were incapable of improvement; they needed only explication and assent. But let experience be put before theology, and religion is no longer viewed as a set of propositions to be defended and believed, but as a great human process—the search after God—and finding Him in a transforming and regenerating experience.

There come certain epochs when a fresh interpretation of religious truth becomes imperative. One of these was in the days of the prophet Ezekiel, when the revolutionary change in the life of the people would have meant the collapse of their faith, but for the fresh interpretation of it which was made by the inspired prophets of the Exile. Another was in the early days of Christianity when the Church confronted great rival systems of thought, and the necessity was laid upon her to expound her faith also "in an order of intelligible ideas." Today we confront a similar crisis, when the trumpet call is heard for the Christian intellect to arise in the interests of the Christian faith. Our environment today is charged with hostile and alien forces. Multitudes of men and women are finding themselves out of sympathy with traditional and outworn statements of religious truth, yet hungry for the truth itself. The high duty is laid upon us to master the new conceptions of nature and of man, and to describe in the light of these conceptions the essence of the Christian experience of God. The provision of such a theology is one of the most impressive demands that is laid on the church in our day. All round us people are asking if it is any longer possible to fit the old traditional theology into the modern scientific conception of the universe; to what extent it is possible for one to hold in sheer intellectual honesty both what modern knowledge teaches us concerning the origin and nature of the universe and what the Bible teaches us concerning the nature of God and of man. The need of a fresh interpretation of Christian truth which shall do justice alike to the revelations of modern science and to the revelation of Scripture is urgent and vital. There are those who say that it cannot be met. But it must be if historical Christianity is to have any future, if the faith of the New Testament, which has influenced the destinies of mankind for two thousand years, is to control the moral history of the race in the ages yet to come.

Indispensable to such a fresh interpretation of historical Christianity is, of course, a thoroughgoing scientific method. The idea that Christian truth is to be preserved by combating science on matters of fact has proved again and again to be pitifully short-sighted Whenever theology has opposed science on its own ground, theology has been not only beaten but discredited. The effort to repeat that experiment in our day has been one of those tragic anachronisms which all true lovers of Christianity deplore. Those who are to write the theology of the future will not hesitate to accept the best and most complete description of the universe which science can give them, confident that they in turn can give to that conception a spiritual interpretation which will satisfy alike the minds and the souls of men. They will leave to the scientists the questions of science. On matters of scientific fact they will express no judgment, for on these matters they are not competent to pass judgment. They will take these facts in so far as modern scientific theory accepts them as facts. And they will use them in presenting to the souls of men, as hungry in this age as in every other for a living God, a faith which is at once adequate to their intellectual ideas and to their spiritual needs. It is where the scientist leaves off that the theologian begins. The theologian waits until the scientist gets through. He never interrupts him, and he never fears him. When he gets through, he has left the theologian plenty of room, plenty to do. For he may have answered the question How? and he may have answered the question When? but he has left unanswered the questions Why? and Whence? and Whither? Theology does not need to dispute science on its own ground, because it has an undisputed territory which is all its own.

In addition, however, to the scientific method, the theologian who is to make for us an adequate theology for the future must possess in full measure the Christian experience, "that good thing, the faith and the love that are in Christ Jesus." Without it, he will never be able to comprehend, and much less to interpret, the meanings of a Christian theology. For if Christian theology is the description of the Christian experience, how can one describe what one has not oneself experienced? One may possess all the intellectual acumen in the world, but one will simply be outside of one's subject. Everything that we call Christian theology is simply an historic attempt at the description of an already existing experience of Christian truth. Consequently no one is really qualified to discern, much less to weigh, the validity of Christian doctrines who himself is a stranger to the experience that produced them.

The German theologian Rothe once made the remark: "It is only the pious subject that can speculate theologically. And why? Because it is he alone who has the original datum, in virtue of communion with God, on which the dialectic lays hold. So soon as the original datum is there, all else becomes a mere matter of logic." [3]

Christian truth, in a word, was given to the world out of a heart that felt itself estranged from God through sin, saved through Christ by Cross and risen life, at peace through Him with God, one's fellow-men, oneself. The knowledge of Christian truth, therefore, can come only with this experience of personal salvation. To have a real competency as a theologian, that is, one must put oneself within the experience that produced the theology.[4] The intellectual form of a doctrine is derived from the scientific mind; but what makes a doctrine religious and Christian is the religious and Christian experience which explains and interprets it. Side by side, then, with the scientific spirit necessary to the theologian is the personal

[3] Quoted by J. C. Shairp, *Culture and Religion*, pp. 124-5.
[4] "It is the heart which makes the theologian. It is a comprehensive and intense Christian experience which alone qualifies a man to attempt with any safety or promise of success the restatement of the Gospel. He must be a scholar and thinker; but what will give worth to all his other gifts is that he should be a saint" (A. E. Garvie, *The Christian Certainty and the Modern Perplexity*, p. 103). A good deal of modern theologizing lacks this indispensable quality. There is much of criticism, science, philosophy; but there is not much evidence that the one who is attempting this restatement of Christian truth has himself experienced the reality which he is attempting to describe, or knows what it is in Christ to have passed out of darkness into God's marvelous light.

experience with which his entire thought and life must be animated. He can be a Christian thinker only on condition that he is first a Christian.

Far from being vague and obscure, to one who is conscious of it the Christian experience is something morally clear and precise. He finds it not only in himself, but in everyone whose consciousness has been awakened to the same life. He finds it in the personal life of every Christian, great or small, illustrious or obscure, and he finds it in the collective soul of all Christendom. This wholly religious and moral consciousness of Christ constitutes and determines what is called, in the language of Christianity, the Spirit of Christ, or God, in the history of humanity. It is a religious sense, a faculty of discernment inherent in the Christian faith, enabling one accurately to appreciate and to judge between all the present and the past, between what is of its permanent essence and what is foreign to it. Outside of this inspiration the work of theology is vain. "Theology abides in its own domain, which is the study and explanation of Christian experience."

We have plenty of theologians who are not doing the work which needs to be done. Some of them are converted men. They know in their inmost souls the realities of the Christian experience. They are filled with a sound evangelical passion, and the truth that they offer in so far as it is religious and Christian both feeds and satisfies the souls of those to whom they minister. But these same men lack a true intellectual training and a sound scientific attitude. They offend the intellectual sincerity of their hearers by disputing with science on questions of fact, and pass on a whole traditional theology with no effort to interpret it or to fit it into the thought-forms of men trained in modern ways of thinking.

On the other hand, there are theologians trained to the

minute in matters of science, who are modern to their finger-tips and who talk with the accent, the vocabulary, and the method of the professor. But they have parted company with the historic Christian tradition; they have forgotten, if they ever truly learned, the deep meanings of a Christian and an evangelical experience of God; they no longer understand the meanings of sin and redemption, of love and forgiveness, and the truth which they offer men lacks the deepest, heart-gripping, soul-saving message of the Gospel.

But here and there in our modern world there are emerging men called of God to interpret historic Christianity in modern language. They are not all professional theologians. One does not need to be a professional theologian in order to teach theology. Every true preacher is a teacher of theology. It is his duty to give to his congregation, as one of the most precious results of his ministry, a theology, a well-understood conception of Christian truth, on which his hearers may safely rest their lives. In season and out of season, year after year, this interpretation is unfolded, expounded, explained, yet not in set discourses. The people will not realize that they are being fed on theology at all. But his teaching, always grounded on certain deep and well-understood principles, will have a permanent constructive theological value. And the man who is doing this is one who is in entire sympathy with the revelations of modern science and also is actually living within the revelation of God in Jesus Christ our Lord.

Only one thus equipped, with both secular knowledge and with spiritual discernment born of the Christian experience, will be able to comprehend and interpret the message of the Bible. For the Bible is more than a record of man's experience of God. It is the record also of a

unique, an authoritative, and a final revelation of the
moral character of God to man. If a Christian preacher
does not believe this, then he lacks the basic belief on
which for two thousand years Christian theology has
rested. It has rested on the idea, to use Maurice's magnificent phrase, that in the Bible we do not have men's
thoughts about God, but we do have God's thoughts
toward men. The Bible is a human book in the sense
that it was written by fallible human beings under normal human conditions. It is a human book also in the
sense that the idea of God in it is a growing and progressive idea which advanced gradually under the guidance of God-inspired men. But it is more than a human
book, and there is something more than the human in it.
The old author of the Hebrews gave us the truth of it:
"God who spake in time past unto the fathers by the
prophets . . . hath in these last days spoken unto us
by his Son." [5] In the Bible, God speaks. He may speak
through men, but He speaks nevertheless. And if He
spake at divers times and in divers manners through the
prophets, He spoke once for all through Christ His Son.
This is the foundation of all Christian theology in the
historic sense of that term. And no man is competent to
be a Christian theologian who takes a lesser or a lower
conception of the Bible than that. For the Christian
theologian the Bible must be a uniquely inspired book,
since it contains, between its covers, the final unveiling
of the moral character of God.

From this it follows that the Christian theologian must
be able to comprehend, to interpret, the revelation of
God contained in Scripture. And for this task a purely
secular wisdom will not suffice. Let one be a total stranger to that experience and, competent as he may be in
other directions, he is incompetent to understand and

[5] Heb. i. 1.

2.1986

to interpret the Bible. Thus it is that a man may be learned in other ways and yet show himself to be an ignoramus when he attempts to expound the Scriptures. He may understand the ways of beetles and may calculate with uncanny mathematical nicety the movements of the planets, and still know nothing, literally nothing, about the Bible. Such a man makes the most grotesque comments upon it. Every time he opens his mouth he proclaims his own ignorance concerning it. The Bible is a description of man's experience of God and of God's experience with men. To understand it, therefore, one must be within that experience. For how can one understand the description if one has no knowledge of the thing described? And since it is the work of the Christian theologian to interpret this experience, it is above all necessary that, with all secular knowledge, he should have a deep inward experience of God. Only to him will the Bible reveal its innermost secrets. Only he will be able to translate these in modern language to the souls of men who hunger for the secret mystery of God in Christ reconciling the world unto Himself.

If this is true of the Bible as a whole, it is supremely true of the New Testament. What we call the New Testament is the splendid report of the most extraordinary experience of God which the human soul has ever known. The New Testament is the product of that brilliant and controlling reality. This being true, we may safely affirm that the final word about the New Testament will be spoken not by criticism apart from experience, but by the criticism of experience itself. The evangelical Christian is no foe to the critic. But he insists that no one can speak the final word about the Gospels or the Epistles unless he shares to some degree the experience of which they are a report and a description. The reality of Christian experience must always underlie criticism or else that criticism will be sure to miss the reality of the New Testament. It is not criticism which tests the reality of Christian experience; rather it is that experience which passes upon the validity of criticism. For the New Testament books, I repeat, did not create the Christian consciousness; rather they were created by it. Anyone can hold the New Testament in his hand. But he only really owns it who has felt its message in his heart; and it may fairly be doubted if a critic whose knowledge of the New Testament is well-nigh totally literary or doctrinaire can ever say the last word about it.

> Can a . . . professor whose devotion to critical research has done admirable and indispensable service for which we are all in his debt, still be trusted to say the final word about a Book whose message is largely personal and spiritual? For the reality of Christian experience is not an affair of the schools and its literary products do not smell of the lamp.[6]

Such men, earnest, devoted as they are, are accomplished experts, as Hermann has said,

> in a piety that is outside of them; but a piety of their own, a religion of decision, seldom emerges into the light of their consciousness. . . . They can wipe the dust of centuries from the words of Jesus. Nay, they can trace for you with a high order His incomparable spiritual style. But they seldom show a sign of concern about what Christ means for themselves. They do not betray that a personal Life bears down on them out of the page of Scripture and, full and warm, conquers them for His own.[7]

[6] "A student modern to the core who could not conceivably take initiation into any mystery seriously, who is not supremely concerned with sin, nor interested in Jesus Christ or immortality, may have contributions of value to make to the study of Paul, but he will need more than genius to be an interpreter of him." (T. R. Glover, *Paul of Tarsus*, p. 74.)

[7] Forsyth, *The Person and Place of Jesus Christ*, p. 132.

Until a man feels that, he is not in a position to understand the Gospels or the Epistles, since the Christian religion can grow only from what a man himself experiences of the present reality of the Person of Christ. That is, a person needs to be converted before he can begin to understand the real content of the New Testament. And let him be truly and thoroughly converted, and he neither dislikes nor shuns, much less fears, the work which he beholds the critics doing. He is interested in the fascinating story of how the early Christian writers found confirmation or illustration of their faith in Jewish ideas, in the contemporary mystery religions, in Neo-Platonism, in Alexandrian philosophy. But the faith itself, that lies beyond the reach of scholar or of critic, however profound, however acute, either to reach or to touch—and all too often beyond their ability even to understand. The dates of manuscripts, the validity of texts, the fact of miracles, the authenticity of sayings—these are become the subordinate questions relating to the human framework of that Life which itself grows brighter, clearer, stronger day by day. And it is in the light of that abundant and transfiguring Life that these questions are finally resolved. The evidence upon which they stand or fall is in the last analysis not textual or literary or scientific, but inward and spiritual. It is the Person of Christ spiritually apprehended in the heart of humanity which retains or repels, authenticates or disproves, assimilates or rejects, the materials relating to His life. The great prerequisite need for a real and permanent understanding of the Gospels is an adequate and thoroughgoing and spiritual apprehension of the Person of Christ.

We find here the answer to the objection of those whose faith is founded on outer instead of inward evidence of the authority of Scripture to what they feel is the un-

warranted subjectivism of those who sift the contents of
their New Testament, accepting this and rejecting that.
On what ground, they say, and by what right does the
modernist say, I accept this miracle of Jesus as genuine,
but I reject that as spurious? Has anyone a right then
to take what he chooses and to set aside what he chooses?
Does not this place the New Testament tradition at the
mercy of the mind of anyone at all? Is not, then, its
essential authority undermined? The answer, of course,
is that "anyone" has not the right to do this. One's
right to do it, and the accuracy with which it is done,
depend upon the reality of his apprehension of Christ;
upon the degree to which he has reproduced within himself the experience of God in Christ of which the New
Testament itself is a product. It is the Spirit of Christ
alone which judges the Book. To possess the Spirit of
Christ is to possess both the right and the ability to judge
the Book. The Spirit of Christ must judge the writings
concerning Him. Anything which seems to contradict—
which seems not to do justice to, which cannot be har-
monized with—the felt life of Christ, the Christian mind
and conscience has a right to challenge. Whether its
judgment be true or false will depend upon the accuracy
and the degree with which the Christian has reproduced
the mind of Christ.

If the Christian experience alone equips a man to be
a competent critic of the Bible, it alone enables him to
interpret adequately the Person of Christ. Since the earliest days the question has been asked, "Who is He that
I may believe on Him?" It is still being asked. In
the midst of all this ferment of discussion He stands,
at once the most approachable and knowable of men.
But the secret of His personality, the real knowledge of
Himself, are not won by discussion from without. He

can never be understood apart from an experience of Himself. Christ is His own interpreter. And He Himself stands apart from and above and out of the reach of any examination concerning His origin or the outward events of His life. The apprehension of a Divine Christ, that is, rests, not upon the validity of a text or the authority of a document. The portrait of Christ itself, just as we have it in the Synoptics, was not constructed out of early documents. It was the marvelous creation of a redemptive experience of His Person. The evangelists did not search the records for the earliest accounts of His Person; they wrote out that record which He Himself had inscribed within. The portrait of Christ, that is, is itself the product of an experience, and there is no true understanding of His real Person short of an experience of His Person.

It may even be asked if pure historical criticism is possible in the case of Jesus. Does He not compel you to take moral and spiritual sides at once, and does not the consequent criticism depend on which side you take? Before we judge Jesus, does not He first judge us? His appeal to the soul comes swifter than our estimate of His Person. He sifts and measures our souls before we so much as begin to sift documents and measure evidence. Criticism is not possible of such a story without a side taken consciously or unconsciously either in faith or unfaith.[8] And the point is that sides were taken emphatically by the evangelists; and that the very Portrait of Christ which we are asked to examine is a product of faith. To understand it, that is, we need the faith. There is no real apprehension of the Person of Christ short of a spiritual experience of Him. A Hottentot, we may say in all confidence, can as truly perceive the meaning of Raphael's Madonna as a man today with all

[8] *Ibid.*, p. 110.

secular and common sense, with all the latest apparatus of criticism and research; but a stranger to the fact of the Christian consciousness cannot hope to understand the meaning of the portrait of Christ. Among the sources of knowledge of the historic Jesus, not the least important and reasonable is that experience of Christ which alone perceived, preserved, and perpetuated the personality of Christ Himself. We will not deny the rights of scholarship; we will welcome every fresh light that research can throw upon the life of Him who was the Light of Men. But we will recognize that, when it comes to the secrets of personality, methods of science break down, and the last word can be spoken only by the human spirit. No man can call Jesus Lord except by the Holy Ghost. That is, behind and beyond the best work of those who approach the examination of Christian truth without themselves having known the reality of the Christian life, there lies that which they can never comprehend. Their work will have an interest for those who are the sharers of this experience, but their work will never have final authority. Christian truth is authenticated by the Christian life. The imprint of the Spirit of Christ alone guarantees the genuineness of any deliverance as to His Person and work. Only the Christian can give us a truly Christian Christology.

It was out of such an evangelical experience of His Person that the Truth, which today we call the Divinity or the Deity of Christ, was born. Consequently it is only within such an experience that it can be understood. To the end of time the doctrine of the Incarnation of God in Jesus Christ will remain a stumbling-block and a stone of offense in the mind of the rationalist who knows nothing of the reality of personal faith in Christ. The New Testament doctrine of the Person of Christ would have been unthinkable to the writers of the New Testa-

ment themselves apart from their experience of Christ
Himself. "The doctrine of the Incarnation, as it is called,
is the theological expression of His salvation, apart from
which it is little less than absurd, and no wonder it is
incredible." [9]

Enter at this point G. Lowes Dickinson for the last
time, and only briefly, for the purpose of showing what
desperate work he makes of this truth as he brings to bear
upon it an enlightened mind without a heart that has felt
Christ's saving grace.

> Again, whatever the Power be that sustains the
> world, we cannot conceive it to be a Person—even if
> we knew what a Person meant. Still less can we
> identify it with the Person of Jesus Christ or feel it
> to have anything in common with the sentimental
> and almost erotic character of most Christian hymns.
> "Jesus, Lover of my Soul!" What! Is the power
> that is supposed to have created the stars and the
> tiger, to be addressed by a pet name? Need I say
> more on this subject? But can I say less? [10]

No, my brother, you could not say more. Neither
could you by any possibility say less. And by what you
have said you have done a vast service. You have proved
that "It is living faith alone that has the promise of understanding the "object of faith." It is only a soul that
feels itself to be saved by Christ that is ever ready to
confess Him to be both Lord and Savior.

> The deity of Christ cannot be proved to either the
> lower or the higher rationalism, . . . either to the
> man on the street or to the professor in his chair, but
> only to the evangelical experience. To the former,
> this would be the last truth he would accept; but to

[9] *Ibid.*, p. 74.
[10] Art. "Knowledge and Faith," *Hibbert Journal*, April, 1908.

the latter, this would be the last truth it would surrender. A theology of the Incarnation must be a theology of the saved. The fulcrum of any vital doctrine about the Person of Christ must be an experimental faith in Him as Redeemer. . . . We do not go to the ordinary able man and propose to convince him by argument consecutive, cumulative, or convergent that Christ is divine. That would be to attempt the impossible. No argument could convince an unsaved Christian that He is, and no argument could convince one who has really experienced His salvation that He is not.[11]

The appeal of the real Christ is not made to the shrewd and the logical; it is made to the heart and conscience in a real experience. It is only on the experience of a Redeemer from eternal death into eternal life that the New Testament witness of Christ rests. And it is only that same experience which has prolonged that witness in the Church. And it is the selfsame experience alone that witnesses to it today.

No man can be trusted to give to the world an adequate interpretation of the Person of Christ who has not experienced in his own soul the uttermost that Christ can do for men. But possessing that experience, and possessing also an adequate secular knowledge of the world in which he lives, he will be able to interpret the Christ of the New Testament in language and thought-forms which men can understand. Then we will have a Christology which is at once intellectually intelligible and morally adequate. We have either the one or the other often enough, but too seldom do we find one which is both.

The Christian experience alone can be trusted to interpret and to do full justice to the Christian doctrine of

[11] See Forsyth, *op. cit.*, pp. 94, 219, 244.

the Atonement. It is not too much to say that the natural man can make little of it. Short of being oneself
a Christian, it will remain an opaque theological wonder.
Hear the language in which it is discussed as an intellectual conception, apart from an inward experience of
its meaning:

> On what ethical basis can it be affirmed that an
> innocent person can assume the guilt of a guilty
> person? How can such a perversion of the actual
> moral situation work the salvation of the guilty
> person? Must not all of this be relegated into the
> penumbra of rejected theological débris? One can
> understand how the guilty often cause the innocent to
> suffer; one can also understand how the spectacle
> of undeserved guilt can work contrition in the
> heart of him who has caused it. But to go farther
> and to assert that the suffering of Christ in some
> way caused a forgiveness by God to become operative
> which otherwise would not have operated,—this re-
> mains to the natural man not only intellectually
> inexplicable, but morally indefensible.

What all such critics of this most ancient of all the
Christian doctrines forget is that what is called the doctrine of the Atonement is only an effort, feeble at the
best, to explain, or at least to express, what was already
an indubitable personal experience. The experience came
first. It is written all over the pages of the New Testament. The Cross for these men was a salvation, not a
mental speculation; and eternal Truth to be known primarily not by philosophical enquiry, but by a heart conscious of its sin, and conscious also of its deliverance from
sin. Because for these men Christ was the only begotten
Son of God, the death of Christ was unique in its relation
both to the heart of God and to the heart of man. This
for them was a fact of experience. The record of it

constitutes the inspiration of the New Testament teaching and preaching. And the reality of it has been the glory of the Christian experience ever since. Each generation has molded its doctrine of the infinite work of God's redemption in terms of its own peculiar experience. The very fact that the Christian intellect has found it impossible to state that experience in any thought-form which has permanently satisfied the Christian mind is only added witness to the elemental nature of that experience. It was a great saying of Lord Balfour: "If the Atonement were not too wide for our intellectual comprehension, it would be too narrow for our spiritual necessities." That is a magnificent statement. The very fact that the Atonement has been proved to be too wide for our intellectual comprehension is of the nature of proof that it is broad enough for our spiritual necessity. Our Lord's work of redemption is larger and grander than our widest and deepest interpretation; and the widest and deepest theory of the Atonement is never anything more than the word signifies—a way of looking at it.[12] Apart from the experience itself, any attempt to describe it will lay itself open to objection and all kinds of secular criticism. No one who approaches this fundamental Christian doctrine with the intellectual apparatus of the schools but a stranger to the experience which produced it will ever be able to understand it. One must be a Christian before one is competent to discuss the subject.

Our so-called liberal and modern ministers need above all to be converted men, so that out of hearts which have felt the salvation of which the Cross is the symbol they may offer it to other men. Nothing is more tragic than the spectacle of a modern minister approaching this the

[12] I "look at it as if the doctrine was like finding names for your feelings" (George Eliot's *Adam Bede*, quoted by H. E. Fosdick in *Modern Use of the Bible*, p. 261).

central mystery and message of the Gospel without having himself had an inward experience of its meaning. He will theorize about it; he will be able to show how faulty all past interpretations of it have been; he will explain it in terms that are modern and reasonable, in terms also that in no manner of fashion reproduce either the language or the spirit of the New Testament. But the power of it and the reality of it he will never be able to describe or to transmit, because these he has never himself experienced. And the theology which he thus offers is not the theology for which this world waits.

In order to get on man needs to realize by a burning inward conviction that there is no element in life beyond the jurisdiction of God. Man must know that God loves him better than he loves himself. No matter how joyous the world may be nor how beautiful, if we know not the heart of this universe in terms of never altering pity and love, there is no foundation for faith or for holiness. What human experience calls for is a God of love who feels and cares—not an absentee potentate, not a God standing apart watching the game of life, out of touch with human suffering, to whom aspiration is alien—but a God who is *for* men, a God tabernacled with men, militantly and agonizingly taking their part, identified with their immediate suffering and problems, and wounded by their sins and iniquities. Out of the depths men have yearned for Him, and apart from this there is no peace. There is the problem. And Christianity returns its answer. The Cross is the sign that this is so. The conviction underlying the whole of this tremendous moral transaction has been from the first that God was in Christ reconciling the world unto Himself. A truth as profound as this has a visible symbol of its reality. Hence the wealth of devotion and of gratitude which the Cross has evoked from the human heart. The Cross has at its heart a collision and a contradiction, but it can extend its four arms forever in all directions without altering its shape. It is a signpost for travelers. Whichever way life leads you, it brings you Home at last.

A ministry that ignores the fundamental craving of the human heart for peace and certainty is simply playing with human existence as we know it. A ministry that seeks to satisfy that craving apart from the answer of historical Christianity, whatever else it may be, is certainly not Christian. The note of authority with which the Church and the Christian preaching have proclaimed that in Him alone is peace has been the secret of their influence and the source of their power. It is the secret today of the mass of the Roman Catholic Church, and the preaching of the Protestant evangelist. No amount of modern scholarship can take the place of a weakened hold of this fundamental answer of Christianity to fundamental human need. And there is no necessity for scholarship to weaken this conviction. On the contrary, the more we know of this terrible and implacable universe in which we live, the more we know of the inexorable facts of human life and experience, the more pressing does this need of deliverance from the tragedy of human life become. Therefore, to repeat in one's own experience the Christian discovery of redemption and salvation through Christ, to announce on the authority of a personal experience which has been verified by two thousand years of history its possibility for every soul of man—this becomes the glory and the power of Christian preaching today.

Another of these great Christian truths which can be apprehended only by sharing in the experience which produced it is the Christian doctrine of the Trinity. The very mention of the word either leaves many people cold

or rouses them to resentment. The suggestion that one
proposes to demonstrate that this metaphysical doctrine
has a vital message for our modern world lays one open
to the charge of being a hopeless medievalist, a theological anachronism. Yet in sheer honesty this ought to be
done. Is there, then, any sense left in which we moderns
can call ourselves Trinitarian Christians? If so, what
is it? Is the singing of our trinitarian doxologies, and
of our trinitarian hymns, "God in three Persons, blessed
Trinity," and the use of our trinitarian formulas—
is all of this pious tradition merely without fundamental
moral and religious meaning? Has the time come when
the trinitarian formula itself ought to be abandoned by
a modern and liberal ministry that prides itself above all
else on sheer intellectual honesty? Here are questions
that demand an answer.

We begin just where we began with the other cardinal
Christian doctrines. What we call the doctrine of the
Trinity is merely the effort to give intellectual expression
to a preceding spiritual experience. Apart from the
experience which produced it, nothing can be made of
the doctrine of which it is the expression. The modern
man, a stranger to this experience, treats the trinitarian
formula as a sort of theological jest. He fails to see how
three times one can by any kind of theological manipu-
lation be made to equal one. Neither does he see what
any arithmetic of that kind has to do with religion. In
a word, he refuses to take it seriously. Others, less superficial in their attitude, remark that the word Trinity
and the idea which it connotes find no place in the New
Testament: the whole subject belongs to a later and less
religiously inspired age. An actual Christianity can let
it alone. Moreover, is not this what the overwhelming
majority of Christians do? Is not this what the preachers do? When did you last hear a sermon on the Trin-

ity? To all of which the answer must be returned, "How then do we happen to have a doctrine of the Trinity at all? And trinitarian formulas, and trinitarian hymns?" There must be something underlying all this. And there is. The Trinity is merely a word which, however, symbolizes a deep and an abiding experience. That experience begins in the New Testament. It is true that the word is not mentioned. But these men who believed in God the Father before they became Christians had had their profound experience of Christ and had been baptized by the Holy Ghost. This threefold experience had been theirs, authenticated in a fashion so indubitable as to leave no manner of doubt in their minds as to the truth. It was inevitable, therefore, that in time the intellectual effort would be made to explain that experience. The explanation demanded that there should be but one God, for these men were Jews. It demanded also that there should be three separate, personal, and historical manifestations of God, equal in origin, in power, and glory, for nothing less would satisfy their experience.

The effort to find a formula which would combine these two ideas makes up the history of Christian theology for the first three centuries. We find the beginnings of it in the New Testament, where the effort is made to relate the Son to the Father. Throughout the whole process Christian thought refused to be untrue to the content of the Christian experience of God, even though the formula could not be found which could adequately express it. These discussions which ended in the Nicene Creed are dreary reading today, unless one has the imagination to look beneath the surface and see the struggle between intellect and conscience, between the insistence on a formula intellectually intelligible and one that is honest in the report that it gives of an actual spiritual experience. Viewed in this light, the history of the Nicene theology is one of the most dramatic in the whole range of human thought. In the end, the formula, Three Persons and One God. This was the Christian experience of God. And so it has remained. The astonishing thing is that it remains today. The formula has never been abrogated. And it still stands today because the idea of God of which the trinitarian formula is the symbol has been tested by experience and found to be the most serviceable, the most practical conception of God that men have ever known.

The fact that there is that about this conception of God which cannot be explained in terms of cold logic has not interfered with its general acceptance.[13] Men have admitted the mystery and granted the contradiction. But they have discovered that by the help of it they can understand everything else. So they have allowed the mystery, and all else has become lucid. They put the seed of this dogma, if you will, "in a central darkness: but it branches forth in all directions with abounding natural health." In these sentences lies the secret of the vitality of the trinitarian formula. Logic and metaphysics can make little of it. But experience has proved its worth, and to this extent its truth. For the man in

[13] "In the most modern of men there is an instinct which tells him that it is mysticism which keeps him sane. As long as you have mystery, you have health; when you destroy mystery, you have morbidity." . . . "The ordinary man has always been sane because the ordinary man has always been a mystic. He has permitted the twilight. He has always cared more for truth than for consistency. If he saw two truths that seemed to contradict each other, he would take the two truths and the contradiction along with them. In exactly this balance of apparent contradictions has lain the whole buoyancy of the healthy man. The morbid logician seeks to make everything lucid and succeeds in making everything mysterious. The secret of mysticism is that a man can understand everything by the help of what he does not understand. The mystic allows one thing to be mysterious and everything else becomes lucid. He puts the seed of dogma in a central darkness; but it branches forth in all directions with abounding natural health."

the hour of his temptation, for the woman in the hour of her peril, for the soul in the loneliness of its grief, and for the sinner in the agony of his remorse, here is the only gospel that is adequate to the task. The final, and perhaps the only necessary defense of the trinitarian formula, is to say very simply that nowadays we need all the God there is. Today it will be found that that church to which multitudes will continue to go, guided and led by an instinct that is profound and inalienable, is not the church which seeks to make religion intellectually most consistent, but the one which holds out a religion which meets the whole moral emergency of their lives. This does not mean that such a religion will be unreasonable, but it may well mean that it will lie beyond logic. Here lies the final authority of the trinitarian theology. It can be comprehended and it can be vindicated within the realm of experience alone. The minister who will best meet the needs of our modern world is the one who by sharing in this experience is able both to comprehend and to present to others this profoundly Christian conception of God. The search for an intellectual formula which will best convey this idea of God to the mind of our age will go steadily forward in the faith that whatever has helped to make men better is always intellectually as well as morally verifiable. But because one cannot find a logical category adequate to describe this threefold experience of God, never will he surrender the experience itself if he understands the strength and power of the Christian revelation.

Neither will one surrender it if he knows anything about the kind of gospel and the kind of preaching that men welcome today. Laymen are not interested in the technicalities of theological discussion. They will starve and they are starving in so far as they are being fed on either metaphysics or negations. Preachers make a vast mistake if they imagine that what modern Americans are waiting for is a kind of liberalized theology out of which all the old Bible elements have vanished. What they are actually waiting for is a theology which retains all of the Gospel truths, uttered by a man who is himself in the grip of their meaning, and uttered in a vocabulary which any educated person can understand. A theology born out of a thoroughgoing Christian experience and directed to the actual moral needs of men is the theology which this age needs perhaps more than any other. It is astonishing with what confidence one can confront any congregation if one knows how to utter the realities of the New Testament experience of God in a language which men can understand.

From this point of view, it is not less theology that we want, but more. So much modern preaching is barren of all real theological implication and importance. We hear much of Christ the Perfect Example, not so much of Christ as the Bringer of Salvation. We hear much of the Gospel as applied to daily needs, not so much of the Gospel that is adequate to our deepest moral needs. We hear much about a religion that is for this present world, not so much of it in relation to any other. In a word, what were the deepest implications of the Gospel for the first century are passed over rather lightly in the religion of the twentieth century. It might almost seem as if we had evolved a twentieth-century religion that had little relation with the religion that is outlined in at least two-thirds of our New Testament. For myself, I feel that this modernized religion is not only inadequate, but positively unsafe.

There are some lessons to be drawn from religious history. A religion which ceases to strengthen the heart and to fulfill the just demands of the human spirit for guidance through the wilderness of this world is doomed. The needs of the worshipers determines in the long run the fate of religions. Worshipers need an everlasting gospel. When a religion loses touch with human nature, then it dies.[14]

The only thing in the world which holds a religion up is the inherent power of its ideas to meet the general human need. The church can no longer depend upon those visible social organizations which have been its closest allies in the past.

It stands or falls upon the power of the faith which it offers to the world. The deepest strength of the church today is in its religious ideas. By the might of them the church conquered the Roman world; by the might of them European civilization was transformed and today they constitute the sword of the spirit.

Instead of being ideas which we cannot get rid of too soon, they appear to be ideas that we cannot recover too soon. Our greatest need is seen to be precisely in the recovery of our grip on those great religious ideas in which our real strength lies. In the strength of those ideas and in that strength alone we can go forward to the conquest of our modern world as confidently as Paul went forth to the conquest of the Roman world. We have a gospel of which we are not ashamed. For we can say with boldness that not the arts, not the amassing of wealth or culture by the population at large, no scheme of political reform, can do for us the work which needs to be done. What we need today is a gospel which goes deep enough and which rises high enough to meet the tragic facts of human life, and answers the tragic facts of human need. And this world possesses no gospel

[14] Josiah Royce, *Problem of Christianity*, Vol. I, pp. 384-5.

suited to such ends and purposes like the Gospel of the Son of Man who loved us and gave Himself for us. "O Timothy, that good thing, the faith and the love that are in Christ Jesus, keep by the Holy Ghost that dwelleth in us."

CHAPTER V

The Christian Experience And The Preacher

I

Much has been said and written about the office of the preacher of religion. Underlying all else there remains the central fact that the authority, the influence, the commanding helpfulness of the preacher will depend directly upon the range and depth of his own personal experience of God and of the work and mission of Jesus Christ. Preaching is simply an effort to give words and outward content to that inward and spiritual experience. A sermon has been defined as the overflow of the soul. If the soul itself be empty, there can be no overflow. A preacher may possess every other qualification. He may have a fine presence, and his elocution may be perfect. He may be well trained and intellectually the master of his subject; he may have a good set of ideas and a healthy grasp of the practical problems with which he has to deal. He may have all this and much else. But if he lacks, or in proportion as he lacks, a deep vital and personal experience of God and of the Christian revelation of God, he is sure to fail as a preacher. For preaching is simply the uttering of one's own experience. And if one has no experience, neither can one utter it.

It is a man's experience of God, and that alone, which should take him into the ministry at all. Much has been written about the shortage of men for the ministry. The figures do not bear out these facts. The present supply of ministers is approximately one in 513 of the total population,[1] while in 1922 there was one church for about 534 of the population. Under these conditions the immediate multiplication either of ministers or churches is not our present need. Our real need is not more ministers, but more ministers who have literally been driven into their calling by an irresistible experience of God. In W. J. Locke's novel, *The Coming of Amos*, a wise bishop remarks: "He is urging me now to smooth his entrance into a theological college. When I see religiosity develop into religion, I'll think about it." The difference between religiosity and religion is the difference between a second-hand or second-rate, and a first-hand or first-rate, experience of God. The preacher begins his real career at the point where he feels that God has chosen him for this particular and peculiar office. There are other ways of being a Christian minister in the sense of being a Christian servant. It is a good thing that a hundred avenues have been opened up in social service, education, and the activities of the Christian associations whereby a man may do much good without entering the profession of the Christian ministry. It is a good thing because, this being so, the man who today enters the ministry may do so, must do so, under the conviction that this and no other form of Christian service can satisfy either soul or conscience. It is a literal reviving of the well-worn word—"a woe, a curse be upon me, if I fail to utter or seek to utter that experience of God which I know within me." This is the kind of minister and the only kind for which we are waiting today.

In this sense a preacher is a man of God's own choosing. One does not choose the office. It chooses him. If

[1] See Robert A. Kelly, *Theological Education in America*, pp. 177-180.

a man is to be a prophet in any real sense, that will be the way of it. That always has been the way of it. You cannot put your finger on a single prophet in the Bible, Old Testament or New (unless he was a false prophet), whom God did not choose to be His mouthpiece. God raised up prophets. That is why there were prophets. Prophets were not self-chosen; they were divinely called and ordained for their special mission. God needed someone to stand before Pharaoh; so he called Moses and said, "Speak unto Pharaoh that he let my people go." At the time of Eli there was no open vision. So the Lord called Samuel and said, "I will do a thing in Israel this day." Amos was tending his sheep in Judah, but God laid rough hands on him and sent him up to prophesy to degenerate Israel. And when one of the greatest of the prophets described how he came to be a prophet, he said that it was as if one of the seraphim had flown to the altar and had taken a live coal from off of it and had touched his lips with it. Yet I like even better and I am moved even more by the experience of Jeremiah whom I have come to regard as the greatest of all the prophets. No minister, young or old, ought to rest until he has gotten at the heart and within the experience of this man Jeremiah. It will do more to humble him, more to embolden him, more to move him and to make him the man he ought to be than the study of any other character in the Bible, save the Man of Nazareth. Paul of Tarsus is the only other preacher that can stand beside him.

In the first chapter of the book which bears his name, Jeremiah himself explains, with an authenticity which only the most lunatic of critics can question, the ground of his religious assurance. It all lay in his experience of God. "Now the word of the Lord came unto me, saying: Before I formed thee in the belly I knew thee; and before thou camest out of the womb I sanctified thee. I have appointed thee a prophet unto the nations." Then, after Jeremiah had protested that he was too timid, too sensitive a person, too lacking in the self-confidence and assurance necessary to so great a mission, God answered him: "Say not, I am a child, for to whomsoever I shall send thee, thou shalt go, and whatsoever I command thee, thou shalt speak. Be not afraid because of them, for I am with thee to deliver thee, . . ." Then there followed what today we should call an actual psychical experience: ". . . the Lord put forth his hand and touched my mouth; and the Lord said unto me, Behold I have put my words into thy mouth." The merit of this description of religious experience is its simplicity. Here are no cherubim or seraphim, as in the case of Isaiah. Here are no visions of chariots and wheels as in the case of Ezekiel. It is so natural, so human, and at the same time so authoritative and so final. There are no theophanies, no "prophet ecstasies." There is something very intimate, personal, tender, and unsensational about this call of Jeremiah. Yet it must have been tremendous in its effect. God henceforth took possession of Jeremiah. Jeremiah from that time on lived, moved, and had his being in his experience of God, "the richest experience of religion known before Christ." To Jeremiah's protest that he was by nature timid came the answer: "Thou shalt go to all that I send thee, and whatsoever I command thee thou shalt speak. Be not afraid of their faces." And he was not afraid of their faces. He preached for over forty years. During these forty years the nation which he loved and strove to save went down to dust and ashes and destruction. During these forty years he himself, a sensitive soul, with love of nature and delight in all simple, human relationships, underwent every vicissitude, loss, suffering, and humiliation which it is possible to conceive. He was not cheered or encouraged by one single ray of light or hint of what we call success. Yet he never faltered. His last sermon, delivered away down in Egypt to a helpless, disorganized band of refugees who in religious panic had taken up the fantastic worship of the Queen of Heaven, has in it the same ring of conviction that was in his first. His "Thus saith the Lord" thundered at the last with the same detonation, the same reverberation, as at the first. Nothing could stop him. Nothing could daunt him. He was a spiritual catapult propelled by an invisible but irresistible spiritual energy. He goes where he is sent, and he speaks what he has been told to say. And he had "great liberty," as the Methodists say, and he exercised his calling with joy and conviction, and disregarded as immaterial any stray things that happened to himself. From beginning to end the career of Jeremiah illustrates the source and the course of the preacher's inspiration. It all lay in his utter and exquisite experience of God.

It is the same today. The only right, as I see it, for any man to take over the prophetic office of the ministry is that God has called him, set him apart, to do just that work. No man has a right to speak for God unless God has chosen him to be His spokesman. To the other offices of the ministry it might seem as if no special summons or special commission were needed. Native ability might seem to suggest that one should be a parish organizer. A liking for people might seem to make him a good parish visitor. An interest in social problems might prompt him to approach them from the viewpoint of the church. A fondness for church services might seem to fit him to lead the service of worship; good voice and diction might qualify him as a speaker. All of these offices of the parish minister might seem to be decided upon prudential considerations of adaptability and general fitness for the work. But when you come to the prophetic office of the ministry, it is another story. No man can speak for God unless God has chosen him to be his spokesman.

It is sometimes said that the reason that more men do not enter the ministry is just because this "call to the ministry" is made so occult and so mysterious. A man, it is said, goes into the law without any special interior experience. He chooses medicine without going through any special spiritual struggle. When he goes in for business, it is without listening for any other word from God than that which is uttered through the thing that God has made him. And the reason why so many men of excellent ability and preparation pass by the ministry is that they are told that God must call them in some special way—and they have never heard such a call. If it were not for the prophetic office of the ministry, one might agree with this. But I cannot get away from the idea that, if a man is going to speak for God, God has got to choose him for the work. I am sorry for a good many people today. But on the whole the man that I am sorriest for is the man who stands before a Christian congregation without feeling that God has put him there. Of all the dreadful things that men have to do, that on the whole seems to me the most dreadful. This must be the reason why so many men educated for the ministry eventually find themselves in some other "line of business." Preaching, without this inward sense of call and commission, is bound to run dry. Sooner or later such a person will find himself solemnly commissioned to give to others a vision without having had one himself.

To say that some personal experience of God, and some sense that God has chosen one for his task, ought to precede and to underlie the work of the preacher of religion ought not to discourage anyone; rather it ought to encourage him. For it is astonishing how even a mustard seed of real experience of God grows in the work of the preacher. The loaves and fishes were multiplied only when the apostles were bent on feeding the people. And the miracle has been reënacted over and over again. No one need be afraid to undertake his task because he feels how inadequate he is when once this experience of God and this call to his work have become his spiritual possession. God always takes care of His prophets. Moses said that he stammered. But if he did, he stammered to such effect that the world has listened to him ever since. Samuel said, "I am but a child"; but as a child he was worth more to Israel than Eli and all his house. Amos said that he was only a herdsman. But God put a sermon into his mouth that has reverberated ever since in the conscience of men. Whom God raises up, He equips. God never chooses a man to be His spokesman and then deserts him.

Akin to this assurance of success is the assurance of reward. There is no joy on earth comparable to that of the simplest preacher of religion who is doing his work from the sense of a divine commission and who is uttering to men the realities of his own personal experience of God and of Christ. There is no instance of an apostle going half-heartedly to his work. Everyone goes as a lover to the place of his appointment.

The Bible preachers were not richly rewarded by men, but they were richly rewarded by God. They did not have much joy of one kind, but they had joy of another and better kind. When I was in college I heard addresses on the advantages of the Christian ministry. Some of these I remember, to my regret. I am glad that I do not remember who gave them. The advantages of the Christian ministry! What were they? I was told that if I entered the ministry I would enjoy a leisure unknown to other professions; that there would be time for reading and for study that other people had to go without; that one was brought by virtue of his position into the society of the best people in any community; that one's income, while small, could usually be depended upon. And that these were some of the rewards of the ministry. Well, over thirty years have passed since I listened to those addresses, and now I am giving one myself. And I turn it right around today. And I say that, if these are the rewards of the ministry for which you are looking, you would best keep out of it. I do not think that it offers any such rewards at all. In many respects, in most respects, the ministry is the least rewarding of the professions; it is the least stable, the most arduous, the most precarious; often the briefest, and the most beset with difficulties of all kinds. Considerations of self-interest do not take one into the ministry; they ought to keep one out of it. Yet when one says "self-interest" it depends upon the self that one means. For there is no calling which so satisfies and fills with the deepest sense of happiness the highest self of which a man is capable than does the office of the Christian preacher. There were a good many dissatisfied people in the days of the prophets; but the prophets themselves were not among them. And there are a good many dissatisfied people in our day. But God's prophets are not among those either. If you want to hear the lyric of the happy soul, listen to the confessions of those whom God has chosen in our own day to speak for Him. I have known a good many of them—speaking for Him amid the loneliness and dangers and depression of paganism; speaking for Him in out-of-the-way, neglected, degenerate communities at home; but I never yet saw a real prophet of God that I did not also confront a supremely satisfied soul. There is no satisfaction like the satisfaction of a human being who stands before a company, large or small, and declares to them the oracle of God which it has been put into his mouth to speak, which issues warm and real out of the spiritual certainty and conviction of his personal experience of God. The humblest preacher in the land if he be that kind of a preacher can know a joy which no one else can know. And from my soul I envy the man who is going to taste it for the first time and know it for what it is.

If it is our experience of God through Christ which qualifies us to be prophets, it is out of such experience that sermons are born. A sermon is the effort to express one's experience of God through Christ. There can be no such thing as a sermon without the experience of which it is the expression. And the skepticism which men feel toward the preacher and about his preaching, if they feel it at all, is in reality a skepticism as to whether the preacher himself has ever had any real experience of that which he is preaching. When that doubt vanishes, when men are persuaded that what the preacher is saying is to him an intense reality born of an experience of God which is indubitable, then all skepticism vanishes and reverence takes its place. What has been termed respectable inefficiency among the clergy is more often due to poverty of inner experience than to lack of technical training. But never yet in the history of the world have men spoken out of the realities of personal experience without getting a hearing. Men may not applaud what they hear; men may resent what they hear; but listen to it they will if it bear the authentic mark of spiritual reality on the part of him who speaks it. Any sermon gets a hearing which is born of a personal experience of God and is brought out of the deepest and

most intimate centers of one's being—which has the
preacher's own personality behind it and within it. It is
recognized then as something real and valid and genuine,
and it has the respect and attention of those to whom it
is spoken. But apart from this experience of God through
Christ on the part of the preacher, though he speak with
the tongue of men and of angels, all is sound and fury.
It really signifies nothing.

A sermon is an attempt to convey through language
the realities of the Christian experience. It is this which
distinguishes it from all other forms of human speech.
A sermon is not an address; it is not a lecture; it is not
an essay. And yet, like an address, it has a theme; like
a lecture, it has development; like an essay it has literary
form and clothing. What else has it? What is it that
makes of it a sermon? It is the mysticism of the Christian experience of God which it seeks to utter and of
which the preacher seems only to be the mouthpiece.
This makes the sermon. This *is* the sermon. This gone,
nothing else really matters; this present, nothing else
really matters either. Preaching is simply the effort to
communicate in speech the mystery of the love of God
in Jesus Christ to others.[2] Unconsciously to themselves,
perhaps, Christian congregations are listening to find
out if the preacher knows anything about it. And if
within and behind his message, giving it form and color
and passion, there is the spectacle of the soul of the
preacher in vital union with God and Christ and able to
report in some fashion what that experience means to
him, then he may stammer and he may falter and he may
seem to fail, but he has spoken with the evangelical note
and accent that alone can satisfy the human heart. The

[2] "When a man has felt God, his neighbors know it. That is
where the true preacher's power lies. Behind all eloquence, all
learning, its secret is in the fulness and fineness of his spiritual
sense" (J. Brierly, *Ourselves and the Universe*, p. 270).

question is whether we, as preachers, have such a first-hand experience of God, or anything like it. The question is whether scientific or evolutionary or philosophical concepts have taken the place of that idea of God which comes out of the heart of a true Christian experience. The question is whether that intimate fellowship with God, that mystical communion with and knowledge of God which is the essence of the Christian experience, has yielded consciously or unconsciously to other lesser and derived ideas of God which are without vitalizing and propagating power. The traditionalist has ground for his fears that a scientific investigation of the origins of the universe and the origin of the Bible has weakened in much modern preaching that immediate conviction of God as a personal and living and loving Power who delights to dwell in the humblest heart, and to draw near to the contrite ones. Often the preacher seems afraid to be too familiar in his language. But the Bible is never afraid. The Bible is not afraid to say that the hand that bound the sweet influence of the Pleiades and loosed the bands of Orion is the same hand that leadeth us;[3] that the same Being that measured the water in the hollow of His hand, weighed the mountains in the scales, and the hills in the balances, is the Good Shepherd who gathers the lambs in His arms and carries them in His bosom. The Bible is willing to assert that not a sparrow "alighteth" without the Father, and that the providence of God runs through creation from the most distant star to the least of His creatures. We need the recovery of a great spiritual authority in presenting this central idea of the Christian faith. We need, with all our tolerance, a fresh conviction of the supreme splendor, the matchless power of the Christian idea of God. We need to come to men out of the abundant experience

[3] Isa. xl. 11, 12.

of the God whom Christ and He alone has declared and
revealed. "What is God like?" said a dying soldier to
his Roman Catholic chaplain. How would you answer
that question? Well, the chaplain did not say that He
was the unmoved mover of the world. Neither did he
say that He was the uncreated essence. Neither did he
say that He was the power not ourselves that makes for
righteousness. Neither did he say that "God is a Spirit,
eternal, unchangeable in His Being, wisdom, power, holiness, justice, goodness and truth." What he said was:
"He is just like Jesus." "O well, then," answered the
soldier, "I am satisfied." And ultimately it will be found
that only that knowledge, only that idea of God which
comes out of the experience of what Christ is, will satisfy
the hunger and the thirst of men for a living God. It
is by the recovery of that personal experience of God,
while holding to all that a rational science can teach us,
that the modern minister will qualify as a spiritual prophet in our modern world.

Preaching that is born of personal experience will always be directed to personal experience. The preacher
who has had his own vision of God will have but one
purpose—to make other men share in that vision. Thus
the preacher, perhaps alone of all men who speak in public, can be personal without any suggestion or hint of
egotism. He is simply trying to tell other men about
how his own experience of God has helped him in his
daily life, that it may help those to whom he speaks.
Preaching, which has experience at the heart of it, therefore, is always trying to get at the heart of the experience
of other men. It is never vague, generalized, impersonal.
It is direct, near, intimate, and deals always with the
realities of daily experience. It is the bringing to bear
the realities of eternal life upon the realities of daily

life. There is where much modern preaching goes for nothing. It does not focus on the real spiritual situations in which men and women find themselves. But all Bible preaching focused on a real situation. It brought a message from heaven, but it laid it right next door to some concrete situation here on earth. And a preacher who speaks out of his own experience of God will speak directly to someone else's need of Him. Instead of rambling allusion and poetical vaporizing, what the preacher has to say will grapple with the real sins and the real perplexities of real people. The spiritual imagination of the preacher sees, detects, isolates these critical hours of personal experience and brings to bear upon them that evangelical experience of God which is his own precious and priceless possession.

That is the great privilege of preaching. It can "make application." It is perhaps the only method of communicating those intimate messages to the human soul which even the closest personal relations do not permit.

> The most confidential friendship will not allow some of the utterances which are the preacher's exclusive privilege. Some things we say to no one and allow no one to say to us. But they need somehow to be said, and we go alone to the books and to the speakers who will say them for our good. There is no privacy equal to that of the multitude, and the oracles that are most secret are those flung into the world for men to hear who have ears to hear.[4]

It may seem to the preacher as if he were talking into space. Yet if he is speaking of the realities of human experience he may be sure that there are those present who are silently appropriating and applying what the preacher is saying to themselves. "The hazard of strong

[4] From an editorial in the *Christian Register*.

truths changes into providence, and . . . human nature is so thirsty and absorptive that not a drop of the water of life goes to waste."

The preacher who thus speaks out of experience to experience, produces the same surprise which the apostles produced at Pentecost. They spoke to a varied and conglomerate multitude. But everyone in that motley throng heard them speak in a language which he could understand. For it was to what was common to them all that the apostles spoke. They did not preach in a dialect which some but not all could understand. Possessed by a direct experience of God, they were enabled to speak in the universal vernacular of the human heart. They uttered a universal gospel that had application to universal needs. It seemed to each one on that day of Pentecost as if that sermon had been preached for him and to him.

Modern preachers who are able to speak out of the fulness of their own experience of God produce the same impression. Their listeners crowd about them when they have finished and say in surprise that the sermon has been fashioned in some strange way to fit their case. The preacher has spoken in their language. But no preacher can use Pentecostal language which is universally understood unless he has had his Pentecostal experience of God. Too much preaching is in dialect. It is the speech which some men use, but it is a foreign language to others. What the preacher above all else needs to learn is the language which everyone understands. But he will never learn it except in the school of Jesus Christ. The Christian experience of God equips a man to speak not with the tongue of men or even of angels, but with the accent of Christ to which every soul makes instant response.

Thus all true preaching is in a sense expository preaching. It is an exposition by the preacher of the Bible experience of God. If a man has enriched his being by a devout and continuous feeding on the Bible; if his sermons are truly Bible-made; if he is giving out richly what he has bountifully taken in, then the power of the inspired writers will have passed into his own being, and out of his being it will pass into the congregation. He will cease to be a man apart, talking from an attitude of intellectual superiority and professional knowledge, and will identify himself all the way through with the people in the pews by the fact of the living communion of his soul with their souls, established by his being the medium of an inspiration coming to him from the Bible and from Him whose life and love the Bible contains and describes. Hundreds of preachers, not gifted in many other ways, but good, devout men, by their intimate and loving familiarity with the Bible, and by their ability and earnestness in expounding the Bible experience of God, have strongly gripped the congregations of their churches. The man who preaches out of his head, whose sermons are largely the fruit of a secular culture, sooner or later gets stale and preaches himself out. It is the Bible preacher, always finding in it inexhaustible spiritual treasure, who keeps himself fresh year after year and never fails to satisfy the human hunger and thirst for God. Dr. Alexander Whyte made it his lifelong practice to use an interleaved Bible. In giving one to his nephew, Hubert Simpson, who had entered the ministry, he used these words:

> I have used such a Bible ever since I was at your stage of study, and the use it has been to me is beyond all telling. For more than forty years I think I can say, never a week, scarcely a day has passed, that I have not entered some note or notes into my Bible. . . . I never come in my reading on anything that

sheds light on any passage of Scripture that I do not set the reference down in my Bible. And as time has gone on, my Bible has become filled with illustrative and suggestive matter of *my own collecting*. The Bible deserves all our labour and all our fidelity; and we are repaid with usury for all the student-like industry we lay out upon it.[5]

Is there any question that if a minister today with all his modern equipment and apparatus, would get as close to the heart of his Bible as this great Scottish preacher kept to his that the deep and eternal experience of God in Christ would possess his being, and through him possess the lives of other men?

The truest and the most fruitful ministry is one that is born out of the "eternal elements of experimental religion." And the finest preaching is that which gives utterance to these realities. The preaching for which we wait here in America is that which is the fine blend of both mind and heart; which is truly rational, in that it is based on the accepted intellectual presuppositions of our modern world; and at the same time is truly prophetic and evangelical, in that it issues from a heart itself in the grip of the Christian experience of God and knows how to utter the reality of that experience so that other men may feel it and know it. This is what we find in the best Scotch and English preaching. It is beyond our American preaching at just this point, and even Americans admit the disparity. Behind Scotch and British preaching there are generations of inherited aptitude. There is always a background of wide reading evidenced not by frequent quotation, but by allusion and richness of suggestion and material. There is always a background also of hard thinking. Evidently the mind

[5] G. F. Barbour, *Life of Alexander Whyte*, pp. 289-290.

has been trained in philosophical method and is fully aware of modern scientific attitudes. Yet with all this there is to be found in much of the best Scotch and English preaching an evangelical fervor, a spiritual passion, a prophetic mood and purpose which grip the heart and make it feel the full impact of the Christian evangel.

Here in America, however, too often we have either the one or the other. We have intellect without passion, or we have fervor without intellect. The weakness in American preaching today is the rift between knowledge and prophecy, between intellect and evangelism, between scholarship and passion.

There can be no question on which side of this line "we young radicals" will be tempted to stand. Our danger is not that we shall be over-intellectualized—no man can ever be that—but that we shall lack that deep inward and spiritual experience of Christian truth which will cause all the intellectual framework of our preaching to become the invisible background of it, while the preaching itself is direct, simple, authoritative, and moving with the fervor of an intimate experience of God and a personal knowledge of the unsearchable riches of Christ. In a word, the danger of the preaching of those of us who have received the best academic training which our schools and colleges can give is not to oversentimentality. Just the reverse is true. There may be those who feel that the danger of liberalism today is that it shall make too much of experience and not enough of the effort to formulate that experience in intelligible intellectual terms.[6] The danger that I see is that so-called liberals will not indeed become radicals, but will become rationalized to the point of becoming strangers to the deep and permanent elements of the Christian experience. Or,

[6] H. E. Fosdick, *The Modern Use of the Bible*, pp. 187-9.

if they are not wholly strangers to these themselves, that they shall not know how to express them.

Much has been said and written about what kind of a theological seminary we need in our modern world. But one can compress the whole subject in two or three sentences. We need seminaries which will send out men who are intelligent, who know the ruling ideas of our modern world, and have a reputable intellectual background in secular science and theological science, in secular literature and in Biblical literature. But we also want seminaries that will send out men who by their own personal and cultivated experience of God are prophets and evangelists. We do not want men who think they know so much, and really know so little, about comparative religion, that they are in doubt about the uniqueness of the Gospel or the supremacy of Christ. Neither do we want men who have so inverted what they have learned of homiletics as to place manner above message.[7] Seminaries and schools of religion that will send out men who are both intelligent and prophetic, who are prophets just because they do know their world, their fellowmen, and their God—these are serving their day and generation as no other institution that is among us.

If a theological seminary has any task or duty to perform, it is to safeguard, to tend, to develop, and to fan into a flame the prophetic gift of those who come to it for light and leading. Of all the criticisms which may justly be directed at a school of religion, the last and the worst is that by any process of uninspired teaching,

[7] "No stilted, timid pulpiteers who have never learned that grace is more than grammar, and that to win your hearers you may break every pulpit convention that was ever designed by a sleek respectability to keep a volcanic Gospel within the bounds of decency and order, will ever capture the soul of a great city and speak with a voice that will ring in the hearts of a free people" (Silvester Horne, *Romance of Preaching*, p. 201).

any overlaying of the conscience with the accumulated dust of the centuries, any technicalities of instruction or absence of the flame and fire of the Spirit of God, in teaching and living, there has been dimmed or quenched the original passion to proclaim the oracles of the living God. We want schools of learning, but we want also schools of prophets. We want schools in which learning and passion are so joined that one speaks alike with the authority of knowledge and with the authority of the Spirit.

For example, many a modern preacher has intellectual scruples born of his scholastic training concerning the words, the vocabulary, which he can honestly use. How can he use words which have become identified with ideas which he no longer holds? And yet there is simply no substitute for certain words, a certain vocabulary for conveying the reality of the Christian experience. How refreshing it is to hear a preacher, whose every sentence betrays his college breeding and academic background, still using the familiar terminology, the evangelical vocabulary, the vocal notes and stops and accents of a truly experimental religion. There is no language that can take the place of Bible language. How refreshing it is to hear a good Methodist speaking of "having a concern"; about having a "stop in the mind"; "they cannot get on"; "the Lord has closed the door." The familiar and tender words of a truly evangelical experience are inimitable in their richness and power and spiritual appeal. The old words, "the home coming phrases," sin and redemption, Savior and salvation, cross and redemption—these have a power of spiritual appeal which any other vocabulary lacks. Even the word "blood," which the modern preacher shuns as he would the Ancient Mariner, is potent in its latent appeal. It is found in certain verses in the New Testament for which there are no substitutes, and in cer-

tain hymns which will never be outworn. Dr. Whyte used
to tell of "Rabbi Duncan of Scotland who once saw a
woman in a seat near the front of the church during
Communion service pass the cup untasted while the
tears coursed down her cheeks. Leaving his place at the
table, the great scholar stepped down into the aisle, and
taking the cup from the elder who held it, gave it himself to the weeping communicant with the words, 'Take
it, woman; it's for sinners.' "[8] The "young modern
radical" has no language to equal this in its appeal.
"It's for sinners" tells the story as it needs to be told.
A preacher may well scrutinize his vocabulary to see
what kind of words he uses. But the words that carry,
the words that find and win the human heart, are the
Bible words that are saturated by centuries of use with
the Christian experience of God. Yet there are modern
preachers who deliberately avoid them. They avoid
them lest they convey a wrong impression or seem to
suggest some discredited theological idea. The notion that
Bible words cannot be used unless one endorses every
theological idea that has been based on these words is
one that needs to be dismissed without delay. I wish
that everyone of us might read a remarkable dissertation
of Horace Bushnell, delivered originally in New Haven
and repeated later in Cambridge, "On the Nature of
Language as Related to Thought and Spirit." It is the
first of three discourses published under the title *God
in Christ*. The thesis of that treatise is that all words
are symbols, and necessarily inadequate symbols; that
it is a profound mistake to accept words not as signs
and images but as absolute measures and equivalents
of truth; that the higher one goes in human experience,
the more inadequate words become to express the reality
of which they are but the symbol:

[8] *Life of Alexander Whyte*, p. 310.

> My dark and cloudy words, they do but hold
> The truth, as cabinets enclose the gold;

that the language of the Bible, the language of Christian doctrine, as well as the language of the creeds, are full of words which not by their literalities, but by what they point to as signs and symbols, seek to express the realities for which they stand; that religion has a natural and a profound alliance with poetry; that all religious language carries in its bosom some flavor of meaning or import derived from all the past generations that have lived in it; that language is rather an instrument of suggestion than of absolute conveyance of thought; that it is incapable of such definite and determinate use as we have supposed it to be in our theological speculations; that there is, in a word, a mystic element in language and also in the views of Christian life and doctrine that follow; that we need the mystic temper to use language aright; that a mystic is one who finds a secret meaning both in words and things back of their common or accepted meaning, some agency of life or living thought hid under the form of words and institutions and historical events; that in opposition to one-sided intellectualism we need mysticism adequately and truly to understand the religious realities which lie at the bottom of the written word—this is the thesis set up and defended by Dr. Bushnell with surpassing force and eloquence.

> When we think of ourselves trying to give out the substantial part of the [Bible] in a few scant formulas . . . it will not be strange if we drop our feeble, bloodless sentences . . . and return, only mortified, into the faith of those august and magnificent forms of Scripture—Incarnation; Father, Son and Holy Ghost; atonement as blood, life, sacrifice,

propitiation, ransom, liberty, regeneration, wisdom, righteousness, sanctification, and redemption—the great mystery of godliness. . . . I make no disavowal, then, of the fact, that there is a mystic element, as there should be, in what I have represented as the source of meaning in language, and, also, in the views of Christian life and doctrine, that follow. The very last thing to be feared is, that our loss-and-gain style of religion, the stern, iron-limbed speculative logic of our New England theology, will receive some fatal damage from a trace of the mystic element.[9]

If for "stern iron-limbed speculative logic of our New England theology," you substitute the words "the rationalized, modernized theology of so-called liberalism," I believe that these words of Horace Bushnell have a direct message to much of the preaching of the present day. We need the recovery in our vocabulary of the familiar symbols of the Christian experience, the well-worn and dearly loved battle-flags under which generations of Christians have fought a good fight and won their victory.

There are two more qualities in the preaching which issues out of the Christian experience of which mention must be made. One of them is that of simplicity. The more deeply evangelical our preaching becomes—the more it springs not out of theorizing about religious truth, or speculation concerning it, or argumentation, or philosophizing, or any such creature, but out of one's own personal experience and knowledge of it—the more direct and simple, the less involved and abstract our preaching will become. And this is the kind of preaching which the people are glad to hear. Preachers who

[9] *God in Christ*, pp. 71, 95-96.

speak from an abundant experience of the Gospel never need to accommodate their preaching to the type of congregation to which they speak. It is not discoverable that Jesus altered his vocabulary, his delivery, or his ideas whether he spoke to Nicodemus, the university president, or to the woman at the well of Samaria. The deepest truths are always the simplest. And it is the deepest truths uttered in the simplest language which men delight to hear. The most intelligent hearers are those who enjoy most heartily the simplest preaching. It is not they who clamor for superlatively intellectual or aesthetic sermons. Daniel Webster used to complain of some of the preaching to which he listened. "In the house of God" he wanted to meditate "upon the simple verities and the undoubted facts of religion," not upon mysteries and abstractions. All great preachers are the simple preachers. The Old Testament prophets were great preachers. But their language is as direct and simple as their message is clear and easy to understand. "I cannot explain just why it is that the true prophet is always a master of simple speech, but it is certain that no man can speak home to the hearts of the people without it." My own explanation is that the true prophet always speaks from experience; and that there is this difference between a logical and mystical apprehension of reality: that the former is labored and secondary and the latter is primary and immediate and simple. A truth that is acquired in a derived fashion will be uttered in an involved fashion. But truth that is apprehended with the simplicity of direct knowledge will be uttered with the simplicity of direct speech. Academic language is the curse and ruin of preaching. You cannot be too simple in your phrasing, whatever you are in thought. You will weary people with high-sounding rhetoric, copious quotation, and vague philosophy. But if you try out of your own experience to speak in language that is simple, in ways that are solid and true. and applied to their experience, people will not become wearied at all. And simplicity of manner may well accompany simplicity of diction. An ancient chronicler thus describes certain preachers of his day:

> Some forward ones moved to violent motions in casting abroad their ideas, smiting the pulpit, lifting themselves up, or suddenly stamping down; others through too great fear and bashfulness which causeth hummings and spittings, rubbing their browes, lifting up their shoulders, nodding of the head, taking hold of the cloke and gown, fiddling with the fingers upon breast buttons, stroking the beard, and such like toile.

It is not "these forward ones" who make the deepest impression. In fact, as a rule, the simpler one's manner, the more effective one's message becomes.

Together with simplicity of speech and manner, however, there always goes in the preaching which issues from experience of God the sure note of authority. That is why Bible preaching comes with authority. The preachers of the Bible are telling things which they know. Their knowledge is positive because it rests on a personal experience of God. It is because people want a message with authority behind it that they love their Bibles. For the same reason they are dissatisfied with much modern preaching. They are looking for someone who can speak with the positiveness of personal conviction. But it is not evident that this assurance belongs to the preacher. He argues, he interprets, he explains; he raises many questions and he raises many hypotheses. It is very plain what he does not believe, but it is not so plain what he does believe, or, what is worse, even that he believes. Without this note of spiritual authority, a sermon may possess all else—introduction, exposition, illustration, application, and peroration—but it has lacked the one thing which gives a sermon carrying power—the breath of the Almighty. Unless the preacher's own soul has been troubled, no one else's will be. Except the preacher has first trembled at the voice of the Lord, no one else will tremble at the sound of his voice. Wherever you have a preacher burning with his message and delivering it as well as a good singer sings, or as a good writer writes, the people are eager to hear. The indifference of the people to preaching is due to the fact that the preaching is indifferent. Once the hungry sheep looked up and were not fed; now they do not look up, they only stay away. A difference, it has been said, between the ancient preaching and the modern is that in the old days preachers could be certain that the people would come back. If people do not come back to the modern preacher, this is one of the main reasons. People do love to hear preachers who mean what they say.

Note that it is only the authority which is born of experience which people love and welcome. All other authority they resent and despise. There is a world of difference between the authoritative and the dictatorial. The authoritative messenger is clothed with humility; the dictatorial messenger is clothed with a subtle pride. The authoritative messenger is conscious that he has been near to the Lord; the dictatorial messenger is conscious of his aloofness from man. The dictatorial is self-raised; the authoritative comes "from above." The reason that the common people heard Jesus gladly was that the authority which lay behind His teaching was His own experience of God. It was not the authority of the scribes who sought to impose conventional practices or beliefs upon the people. There is, as we all know, a positiveness which irritates people. They feel like say-

ing, "How do you know?" "Who told you so?" It is
the conviction born of experience, and not the dogmatism
of opinion, which makes preaching effective. Let it be
evident that one is speaking with conviction what he himself has learned to know of God, and though men dis-
agree with his opinions, they will listen to what he has
to say. There is all the difference in the world between
intellectual dogmatism and spiritual assurance. The
former is always based on some theory of the truth, but
the latter on the truth itself; dogmatism always insists
on definition, but conviction is born of the reality which
underlies the definition. The one is a matter of opinion,
but the other of experience.

All utterance that is born of experience or persuasion
within it is like a burning and a shining light. It is
always clear and positive. Bible preaching is always
positive because it is the utterance of a first-hand experience of God. When Moses stood before Pharaoh
and prophesied, Pharaoh knew, when he had finished,
what Moses had to say. When Nathan stood before
David and said, "Thou art the man," David was in no
manner of doubt as to what he meant. When Elijah
had finished his sermon to Ahab, Ahab did not have to
spend much time making up his mind what Elijah was
driving at. After Amos had finished his sermon at Bethel
by saying, "For three transgressions of Israel, and for
four I will not turn away the punishment thereof; I hate
and despise your feast-days, and I will not smell in your
holy assemblies; but let judgment run down as waters,
and righteousness as a mighty stream," the people looked
at him in anger, but not in doubt. When Jeremiah stood
before Jehoiakim and preached, there was no question
about what he believed. All of those sermons were like
projectiles. They had behind them the power of a passionate conviction born of an experience of God.

It is just so in the New Testament. No one can read the New Testament preaching without discovering the surprise, the joy, the romance of it. It was a proclamation of good news which the preachers had discovered for themselves and were bent on announcing to the people. They were witnesses of these things. We cannot *but* speak, they said, the things that we have seen and heard. Always it is their own experience of God in Christ which underlies their preaching and gives it its note of assurance. "We know," says Paul; and preaching becomes effective the moment that the preacher can say that he knows, the moment it is evident that this knowledge is born of his personal experience of God.

Luke, the companion of Paul, tells us that "when Silas and Timothy came down from Macedonia, Paul was constrained by the word and testified.[10] So, according to Luke, on this occasion, at least, Paul was "gripped" by the Word. It was not he who had the Word; the Word had him. Into this preaching Paul was thrust by the constraining power of a great conviction. This phrase vividly suggests the ideal condition and experience of a real preacher, and unless he is somewhere near this condition his ministry will be a failure, with little or no joy or fruit in it. All true preachers have this sense of urgency behind them. Martineau used to go to hear Spurgeon preach. A friend asked him why he did: "You do not believe a word that he says." "No," replied Martineau, "but he does." The secret of the carrying power of all true preaching lies in the experiential quality of it. It is this which gives it its prophetic note. Once let preaching become the irrepressible utterance of an inward experience of God, and you begin to hear the boom of Old Testament artillery, the reverberation of a prophetic message, and a New Testament Gospel which has within

[10] Acts xviii. 5.

it the severities of justice, but also the grand sweep of redemption. Without passion no pulpit can be a throne of light.

Walt Whitman in his "November Bough" describes the effect upon him of the preaching of Father Taylor, as he was known, for years chaplain of the Boston Port Society, a mission for sailors:

> I repeat and would dwell upon it, among all the brilliant lights of bar and stage, . . . I have never heard anything in the way of vocal utterance to shake me through and through . . . like these prayers and sermons; like Father Taylor's. *personal electricity.* . . . Never have I heard such impassioned pleading, such human harrowing reproach, such probing to the very depths of conscience and remorse which probably is in the background of every life, every soul. For when Father Taylor preached or prayed, the rhetoric, the art, the mere words (which usually play a big part) seemed altogether to disappear, and the *live feeling* advanced upon you, and seized you with power before unknown. Everybody felt this marvellous and compelling influence.[11]

It is the "personal electricity," the "live feeling," born of a personal experience of God and directed to the realities of human experience which makes a real sermon. It is this evidence of genuine sincerity and passion which gains for a preacher the confidence and response of those to whom he speaks.

Theology, it has been said, has nothing to do with the fulness and emptiness of a church. This has all to do with the personality of the man in the pulpit.

If he is a good speaker and otherwise interesting in himself, he will have plenty of hearers. He can

[11] Quoted by Samuel Eliot Morison in *Maritime History of the United States*, pp. 250, 252.

preach what he likes doctrinally and people will listen. If he has no popular gifts he may be the possessor of all the wisdom of the ages, but he will be left to waste his sweetness on the desert air.

There is much in this paragraph with which I am unable to agree. Theology, it will be found on closer examination, has much to do with the fulness and emptiness of the churches. If you will look to the churches that are full you will find some fulness of theology inside of those churches. It is precisely the fulness of Him which filleth all in all.

Yet it is doubtless true that the personality of the preacher has much to do with the effectiveness of the message which he brings. It is a mistake, however, to call this endowment by the term "popular gift." That is precisely what it is not. It is not a popular gift, it is a divine gift. People see through "popular gifts," but they see into the divine gift. The endowment which makes the personality of the preacher effective is the directness and reality of his experience of God. If the preacher is to preach holiness, he must himself desire holiness and must impress his hearers as one who is seeking after it. Any hearer of keen moral sensibility is a judge of the preacher's moral quality, whether lofty or low, and the impression left will vary even when there is no conscious judgment. The one fundamental and indispensable prerequisite of the preacher is to possess and to give daily and hourly witness to the fact that he possesses a personal and intimate experience of God in Christ. That will lend to his words a sincerity, an authority, a passion, which no external art or training can bring. "O Timothy, that good thing keep by the Holy Ghost which dwelleth in us."

CHAPTER VI

THE CHRISTIAN EXPERIENCE AND THE PREACHER

II

IF PREACHING is the effort to put into speech one's experience of God, it follows that the preacher will begin to speak at the point of his own experience and never utter anything that lies outside or beyond that experience. It will be only what his eyes have seen, his ears have heard, that he will declare. Everyone when he begins to preach must have something in which to believe, behind which he can put all the soul that he possesses. Some vision of truth is his own. And this he will declare. Never for a moment will he allow the expression of truth to go beyond his own personal apprehension of it. The foe, it has well been said, which lies in wait for the preacher is unreality. A very competent authority, himself on the inside where he can observe, has said that the two besetting sins of the ministry are laziness and lying. By lying he means the essential thesis of unreality. The moment a preacher begins to declare something which he has read about, which he has been taught about, which someone else has preached about, which he has every good reason to believe people ought to know about, yet something which lies outside and beyond the range of his own personal experience—that moment preaching becomes unmoral, if not positively immoral.

It is by preaching what we do believe, and only what we believe, that we discover more truth in which to be-

lieve.   The experience of God out of which we preach
is never a stationary thing.   It grows daily and hourly.
Paul spoke only what he knew.   But how that knowledge
of God in Christ grew from the first preaching which was
all wrapped up in Jewish ideas and figures of speech
to the glorious liberty of the Gospel at the end of his
life!   You will not find one idea in the whole of the
theology of Paul which did not change and advance as
he himself pressed onward and forward into his fuller
experiences of Christ.   Every preacher worthy of the
name will have the same spiritual history.   He will speak
only what he believes.   But as he does so the range and
depth of what he believes constantly increase.

Preaching that is born of experience is always fundamental preaching.   That is, it places every special problem in the light of eternal truth.   The preaching is central
and not peripheral.   There is never anything temporal
or trivial about it.   There is a suggestion of the
inexhaustible resources of a life which has come into
personal knowledge of the realities of experimental religion.   The hearer is always made aware by everything
the preacher says of this great hinterland.   Such preaching has within it unspeakable reserves; it has eternity
in its heart.

There is a kind of modern preaching which is the opposite of all this.   "It is lucid, facile, attractive, but it
does not issue out of the depths, and it affords no
glimpses into either heaven or hell.   It does not presuppose . . . one solitary experience of the deeper sort."[1]
Its style may have the secret of the happy touch and
the just word, but passion and greatness it discards.
There are too many preachers who roam over the sur-

[1] Quoted by P. T. Forsyth in *Christian World Pulpit*, from
"Constructive Quarterly," April 19, 1916.

face of Christian truth instead of plunging to its center. We have, too often, the "thin skimmed milk of the word."

When we turn from the facile and winsome, or from the petty and superficial preaching, of which we have so many depressing modern illustrations, to the Bible preachers, we find ourselves in a different atmosphere. I take up, for example, the sermons of Jeremiah. I commend them to you as models worthy of your study. The man has style. But he has something more. If he has something to say that his style cannot express, so much the worse for his style. The Quina rhyme suffers enormous damage in some of Jeremiah's sermons, and the versifiers have a harder time than cross-word puzzlers trying to fit his dynamic utterance into the requirements of scansion. The man has gentleness and sensitiveness; he has love of nature and the tender relationships of life. He has enormous funds of pity and cries out against the cruel compulsions of God that drive him to his task of predicting punishment and disaster to his people. He has love so abounding that he chooses to share their suffering rather than to enjoy the favor of Babylon. But above all else one is made aware in Jeremiah's preaching of the absence of anything that is easy. His sermons come strong and full from an abounding experience of God, and they bring that truth to bear full and strong upon the actual experience of the people. Always it is a high theme. Always it issues from a high experience of God and leads to a high experience of God.

Or, if we look to the New Testament preaching, how rich, how full, how satisfying it seems. It has range, vastness, radiance. There is a manifold glory about apostolic preaching. No wonder that it awoke the wonder of men then, and has remained the inspiration of the church ever since. To reproduce that kind of preaching it is necessary to reproduce the experience of God that lay behind and beneath it. One's preaching will correspond in its breadth and depth to the depth and breadth of one's experience of God. As one knows more and more of the meaning of that experience, his preaching will develop bulk and girth and content, and he will thicken every sermon with an evangelical richness.

I recommend to you the reading of Bishop William A. Quayle's *The Pastor-Preacher*. You will make the acquaintance of a helpful book, but you will also make the acquaintance of a great soul. Only Methodist culture, perhaps, could produce a man like Bishop Quayle—and only one of him. Hear what he tells us about the largeness and size of our sermons:

> Preaching is the art of making a sermon and delivering it? Why, no, that is not preaching. Preaching is the art of making a preacher and delivering *that*. Preaching is the outrush of soul in speech. Therefore, the elemental business in preaching is not with the preaching, but with the preacher. It is no trouble to preach, but a vast trouble to construct a preacher. What, then, in the light of this, is a preacher's task? Plainly this, the amassing of a great self, so as to have something worth while to give. The sermon is the preacher up to date. All his life flowers in what he is saying at a given time. No man can say bigger than he is. He can borrow big phrases and tell them; but their vastness is not his. When a planet swims into the sky it grips other planets solely in proportion to its bulk. Gravitation works directly as the mass. So does the preacher. He must have bulk. He must have greatness.[2]

There is a direct connection between great themes and great ministries. If you will render account of the preachers who have long and fruitful ministries you will

[2] Pp. 363, 368.

find that almost invariably their preaching is on high
subjects, far removed from the trivial, never degenerat-
ing into superficial comments on current events. It has
fulness and depth to it. You may or may not like the
preacher's theology; but you cannot get away from the
greatness of what he has to say. It is not only that the
subjects are great, like Spurgeon's sermons on "Accepted
in the Beloved," "The Glory of His Grace," "Supposing
Him to be the Gardener," "The Exceeding Greatness of
His Power to-us-ward who Believe." But the preacher
is so under the domination of the inward experience of
God that every apparently simple division of the sermon
is "like the turning of the telescope to some new galaxy
of luminous wonders in the unfathomable sky." The
preacher who is fed by this enlarging experience is always moving in a vast world, the solemn greatness of
life is continually upon him, and there is the call of
the Infinite even in the practical counsel concerning the
duty of the immediate day. It is always deep calling
unto deep, the preacher uttering the deep things of God,
and finding response from the deep places of his hearers' life.

A modern reviewer of recent volumes of sermons by
English and Scotch preachers asks the question: "Is our
preaching in America seeking or avoiding high planes
and great and difficult themes? We get the impression
that the English and Scotch preachers are constantly endeavoring to understand and proclaim the meaning of
the Cross of Christ," that is, the center and secret of
the Christian experience of God.

It is this note of vastness, this ever-present sense and
suggestion of the Infinite, which we need to recover in
modern preaching. Bishop Gore once said that the peril-
ous tendency of Protestant ministers today is that they
are seeking refuge from the difficulties of thought in the

opportunities of action. That is a very serious suggestion. It would mean that we are so busy in the shop
that we never had a real view of the everlasting hills.
And it would mean something more. It would mean that
our action will in the end become superficial and ineffective. "A skimmed theology will not produce an intimate philanthropy. We are not going to become more
ardent lovers of men by the cooling of our love for God.
You cannot drop the big themes and create great saints."

Above all, we shall have to fall back on the great
themes if our preaching is to bear the test of being valid
aids to daily living. Preaching, real preaching, ought to
come always to the aid of the struggling soul of man. It
must throw itself on the side of the beleaguered, baffled,
bewildered soul and help it to light, to self-knowledge,
and to victory. Here in the society of Christ divine
forces are leagued and focused which decide the destinies
of individuals and of nations. Within that congregation
men are being braced up for big renunciations and sacrifices. The voice from the pulpit is the ally of the trem-
bling and fainting soul that is at the point of giving up
the battle for righteousness. There the lame must consciously struggle to their feet again. Nothing can do
this work in the realities of human experience except
preaching that has come out of the reality of the experience of God-saving power through Jesus Christ.

The preacher who habitually dwells on the great themes
of the Christian experience is forever delivered from
the danger, into which many preachers fall, of becoming
the victim of his hobby. We have too many hobby-
riders in the pulpit; too many preachers who make the
fatal mistake of interpreting the whole Gospel in the
terms of one solitary idea. It may be a good idea. It
may be a noble idea. But no one good and noble idea

is good and noble enough to exhaust the content of the Gospel, and every preacher should be on his guard against allowing one interpretation of the Gospel to monopolize his comprehension of it. Without doubt this by-product is a precious one; one that has been overlooked; one on which special emphasis needs to be laid; one which has a real mission to perform. But to exalt the derived truth to the place of the source of all truth, to declare a consequence of the Gospel to be that Gospel, to make one of the manifestations of Christ to be the power of Christ— this can only result in mental confusion and spiritual debility.

Now what is going to save us from following too far these excursions and becoming victims of religious fads and fancies? It is by keeping our experience of God in Christ full and complete. It is upon a depleted spiritual constitution that these ideas fasten. One needs always to keep in firm and solid spiritual health. Paul was never weary of urging this upon Timothy. The world was filled with one-sided ideas of Christianity then as it is now. And Paul warned Timothy to lay such hold on the fundamental experience of God in Christ that this would interpret itself in a hundred forms instead of in one. Few counsels to preachers today are worth more than this. It is an achievement in this day of theories and nostrums to walk through life level-headed. But the preacher must be capable of this high performance. Nothing will enable him to do it save such a personal appropriation of the original and inclusive experience of God that will forever deliver him from any partial expression of it. The preacher who has the Christian experience of God for his permanent possession will never mistake the proclamation of fantastic and far-fetched notions which have no real proportion, no adequate basis, as the preaching of Christ's Gospel to man. Too many preachers today mistake the by-products of Christianity for Christianity itself. Or they try to lead their bewilered congregations along the byways and to explore the side-issues instead of keeping to the highway and preaching the main issues, in the light of which alone every special problem of life can be solved. Some ministers go in for social economics; some for psychotherapy; some for menti-culture, while still others aspire to be psychiatrists. Hardly have we absorbed one of these ideas than another is exalted as the real aim and mission of Christ. Now the church appears to be a kind of social laboratory; again it is transformed into a clinic. The message of the preacher, instead of being the utterance of that experience of God which is universal and eternal, becomes the propaganda of the popular theory or idea of the hour.

Such preaching suffers from the want of variety. A minister conceives of the Gospel in certain terms, and he comes to the point where he can present it in those terms and in none other. Small wonder, then, if congregations become restive. The note that he sounds may be a good note and a noble note. But even a good and noble note if sounded too long may get on one's nerves. If I should hear an orchestra strike a beautiful chord and hold it for a whole evening, it would cease to be beautiful. Many ministers commit professional suicide at just this point and then imagine themselves to be martyrs. They think they have suffered as a result of their moral fearlessness; as a matter of fact it is as a result of their wrong-headedness. It is not because they were so brave, but because they were so foolish. I have watched a good many men succeed, as we say, in the ministry, and not one of them was a trimmer; not one of them who hesitated to declare the whole truth of God as he saw it and knew it, or to take the side that seemed "wrong to man's blindfold eye." And I have seen some ministries die violent deaths; and I can say, almost without exception, it was not the congregation that impaled the minister, it was the minister who immolated himself. It was not a case of martyrdom. It was a case of harikari pure and simple. The man did not die speaking for God; he perished thinking of himself.

Some people insist that a man does not have a chance in the ministry to speak out the truth; on the contrary, it is the only chance he has.

But a sense of proportion is needed. A man has become convinced of the social implications of the Gospel. And he is right. The Gospel, once understood, is seen to have tremendous social implications; vast and disturbing social ideas lie embedded within it. But our preacher, once convinced of the social message of the Gospel, begins to utter it. And he keeps on uttering it. And by and by his congregation begins to get restive. They are becoming restive not because of what he says, but because that is all that he says. The pulpit is the grandest, freest rostrum on earth. A parish minister might seem to be the hired chaplain of the people who pay him. As a matter of fact, he never thinks of it; and what is more, they never think of it. He is set apart to declare the words of God, and if he does this with courage, but also with common sense, he will never need to look upon himself as a martyr. A congregation, except in the rarest instances, does not dismiss its minister because of what he preaches, but because of what he does not preach. He has forgotten that the Christian message is a many-sided affair. He has forgotten that the Christian experience of God is rich and varied in its content. The Gospel does have social implications. And freely and fearlessly the preacher will declare them. But social implications are not all that the Gospel has. Jesus was not primarily a reformer, but a revealer; not an agitator with a plan, but an idealist with a vision. The Gospel is not first of all social improvement, but spiritual redemption. Hence, after a sermon on the social aspects of the Gospel, the preacher with a due sense of fitness and proportion will preach one on its spiritual aspects. He will vary the demand for social reform with the special message of spiritual renewal. A preacher who understands the height and depth and length and breadth of the love of God in Christ Jesus our Lord can never remain over-long in any one section of that ample and inclusive experience. The best preaching, as Dr. Cadman has reminded us,[3] resembles a cathedral in which several types of architecture blend together. It corresponds with the different motives that bring men to Christ. It is inclusive in its reach. It strikes the varied notes all of which in harmony make up the "music of the Gospel" which "leads us home."

Preachers who are in earnest in their endeavor to present the permanent aspects of the Christian experience of God to their congregations will find a powerful aid in the Christian Year. Preaching to be constructive and educative must have some deep connecting bond Sunday by Sunday. It is probably a mistake to have too many "series" of sermons. The courage of a congregation often falters as it surveys a long list of projected discourses published in advance.[4] The element of unexpectedness and surprise is a real aid to a preacher. It was once said of a well-known preacher that no one knew

[3] *Ambassadors of God*, pp. 284-285.
[4] It is well also to avoid too many headings to a sermon. "One is warned by the collapse of Mrs. MacFadyen, described by Ian MacLaren. That hitherto unconquered sermon-taster succumbed before the preacher who, after three hours, 'the moon having already risen,' began his last head with the remark: "We will now study Satan in all his offices and characteristics."

what he was going to preach about until he gave out his text. And a member of his congregation added, "And no one knows even then." Yet beneath what might seem to the casual observer to be an unrelated set of sermons, a more careful scrutiny will reveal a well-laid plan running through the whole preaching year, constructed with a view to doing justice to all aspects of the Christian life and experience. All preaching should have the thorough education of a congregation in view. The sermon itself may not be informative or didactic, but when the parish preacher has finished the parish year it will be found that there has been balance and proportion in his work, and that a profound and thorough piece of religious education has been accomplished for his congregation.

To this end the Christian Year is an invaluable aid. If a preacher once learns to follow it he will never fail to do justice to the deep, underlying elements of the Christian faith. Advent, Christmas and Epiphany, Lent and Easter, Whitsunday and the Trinity season, these seasons and festivals all suggest the deep and underlying truths of historic Christianity. They bring to the foreground of the preacher's mind the fundamental and too often neglected aspects of the Christian faith. They cause the preacher to grapple with the great doctrines of the Incarnation, the finality and universality of Christ, the Cross and its meaning, the Resurrection and its social implications as well as its personal consolations. For the Resurrection of Christ not only attests the survival of the individual after death it celebrates also the victory of the spirit in its age-long duel with a hostile world.

The two great festivals which close the Christian year Whitsunday, the day of Pentecost, and Trinity Sunday bring to the front two great Christian truths which the preacher might otherwise neglect or shirk. Indeed the

neglect of these two great themes constitutes a fundamental weakness in modern American preaching. It
is not too much to say that many a preacher does not
know what to do with them. So he lets them alone. As
a consequence, our congregations may believe in God
the Father, and in Jesus Christ His Son, but they do not
know in what sense, if any, they believe in the Holy
Ghost, or why they call themselves Trinitarian Christians
at all. It is a scandal that Christian people are not better
informed and instructed in these fundamental truths
which they profess to believe. "But how shall they believe in him of whom they have not heard? and how shall
they hear without a preacher?" [5] If a man attends an
evangelical or a trinitarian church he should know why.
And that reason should go deeper than the chance popu-
larity of a preacher or the fact that one's friends happen
to attend the church that uses the trinitarian formula.
We need more instructed and intelligent Christians, men
and women who can stand up and give an intelligible
reason for the faith that is in them. But this type of
Christian can be produced only by a preaching that year
in and year out does justice to all of the essential elements of the Christian faith, and above all never neglects
the profoundest of them all. We do not have enough
of such preaching. It is not easy work, it is hard work.
For it does not consist in rehearsing the arguments we
have heard in the classroom or read in our outlines of
theology. It consists rather in putting into speech what
Christ means to *us* as the New Testament describes Him:
the only begotten Son of God, the express image of His
glory, the Word made Flesh.

Thus the Christian Year comes to the aid of the preacher who seeks to do justice to all aspects of the historic
Christian experience. I quite agree with a writer who has

[5] Rom. x. 14.

said that "if the nineteenth century had closed without it, and some earnest and devout soul deeply conscious of the present spirit of unbelief and ignorance of even the salient facts of the Christian faith had, at the beginning of the twentieth century, originated such a plan of annual memorial days and seasons founded on the life of Jesus and the teachings of Scripture, it would have been hailed with enthusiasm." How much more should it be gratefully used since it is the inheritance of the ages, and brings us at once into fellowship with the whole Church Catholic. At least this may be said: a preacher who year in and year out fashions his preaching upon the full content of the Christian faith as it is developed in the orderly procession of the Christian Year will never be trivial or superficial or one-sided. His congregation will be well taught. He will be a workman who needs not be ashamed. He will have faithfully preached the Gospel which is exceeding broad and deep.

In the long run it will probably be found that the deeply evangelical preaching by ministers, who are at the same time truly educated in the secular disciplines, will do more to solve the specific religious problems of any particular group of men than preaching which attempts to do this by the direct approach to these problems. At the present time, for example, people are greatly concerned about a possible and intelligible reconciliation of science and religion. Is it possible for one trained in the modern scientific conception of the universe to embrace in entire intellectual sincerity the truths of a revealed religion? Without doubt, the situation is acute. Many are stumbling and are erring concerning the faith. Multitudes of young men and women, trained in one way in their churches, confront a wholly different set of hypotheses when they enter the classroom in their colleges. They are bewildered and discouraged and they know not which way to turn.

How, now, is a preacher best to meet a situation like this? How is he most likely to help men and women who are asking in all seriousness if they can retain their intellectual sincerity and at the same time their membership in churches which they "joined" before they faced the intellectual difficulties which "faith" seems to involve? The situation will not be met solely by preaching sermons on science and religion, on evolution and Genesis. Without doubt such sermons ought to be preached. The ground ought to be cleared of any preliminary confusion of ideas. In this way certain questions can be answered; some concrete difficulties may be overcome. But the thing and the only thing which will eventually free the mind and the soul from every last lingering doubt, and endow it with freedom, assurance and joy, will be by transmitting to it the secret of an immediate, personal experience of God. In the light of that experience, that contact with reality, in the light that thus shines not only upon some aspect of the subject, but illumines the whole soul, difficulties will pale, shrivel into insignificance, and ultimately disappear.

A practical proof of this is seen in the rapid way in which all apparently insurmountable intellectual difficulties vanish from the minds of the most skeptical the moment these have been gripped by an actual experience of God. Cases abound. They are coming to light every day. A much read book today is entitled *Except Ye Be Born Again*, written by a member of one of the most cultured of our New England families. Mr. Cabot, before his conversion, found Christian things to be unreal. They simply had no meaning to him, no practical influence or control over his life, his motives, his actions. Then followed his conversion, which consisted in an immediate, a personal, a vivid experience of God. Thereupon his intellectual difficulties were not so much solved as dissolved. They faded in the light of this new experience of God. The preacher who will do the most to meet the intellectual problems of our modern world is one who himself has the fullest and deepest experience of God, and knows how out of its fulness to bring it to bear upon other men's lives. The sermons that will do the most to solve men's intellectual doubts are those which, issuing from the depths of spiritual experience, create an atmosphere of such spiritual reality that in it these doubts are dissolved and the soul knows because it sees the truth.

It is not argument that people most need. They need to be confronted with spiritual reality. Then argument ends. The fact is that many people are suffering from an exclusive or one-sided intellectualism. It is a malady often met with in our modern world. It is not the way to deal with these people, to give them argumentative discourses or books on "evidences." They will be sure to come back at you, *riposte.* They are more or less adept in this kind of theological fencing. Even at the best, a provisional, a tentative, a possible agreement is all that will be won. The only ultimate cure of unbelief, it needs to be remembered, is the cure of the nature which harbors it. What these people need is not less intellectuality, but more, much more of spirituality. Preaching and reading which quickens and rouses the dormant spiritual faculties will do more and go farther than any amount of argumentation. Thus the reading of biography is often the best antidote to an intellectual sophism. I rarely prescribe any other kind. It confronts one with the real thing in religion: with a godlike human soul, and then there *is* no answer. There is a reality which is not arguable. Thus it is not by argument or logical device, not by demonstration drawn from secular knowledge, that faith is given to man. It is not taught, it is caught: caught from contact with some soul which itself possesses in large measure the experience which it seeks to transmit to others.

If this is true of the intellectual problems of our time, it is also true of the social problems.[6] It is a mistaken notion that the preacher who is doing the most to help us to Christianize the social order is the so-called "social" preacher, whose sermons bristle with the discussion of the so-called social question in all of its different phases. Society, it needs to be remembered, is always the illustration of underlying and tacitly accepted ideas. The real way to change society is to change the ideas upon which it reposes. All preaching that has actually resulted in improved social conditions has been drawn not from textbooks on economics, and not from contemporary theorizing concerning social needs. It has been drawn out of the deepest and broadest possible experience of God. The preacher who lacks that experience may state his views on this or that subject and take sides on this or that aspect of social or international relations, but he will make little impression either on the minds of his hearers or on the mind of his age. But the preacher who, delving beneath all the current industrial or political questions, declares the whole oracle of God, and presents week by week an authoritative, searching, and uncompromising announcement of the underlying spiritual principles of the Christian evangel, will be making a distinctive and profound contribution to the solution of every problem, which today vexes our social conscience. Prohibition and child-labor, poverty and crime, war and

[6] For a full discussion of this subject, the reader is referred to the author's *The Christian Church in the Modern World*, Chapters IV and V.

international relations, these all will find themselves set down against the eternal background of a profound experience of the life and love of God in Christ, with all that it implies in social relations and in social conduct. It is for spiritual prophets that the times call, for men who see into the deep things of God and by their faithful witness create new and better ideas, and create new and better men and women who will see that those ideas prevail.

The age in which we live offers an unparalleled opportunity to the truly spiritual preacher who speaks directly out of his own Christian experience of God. Sometimes we are told that the opposite of this is true. We are reminded that the church has to face a keener competition in our day than in any previous age of history. Never were opportunities so abundant for a profitable enjoyment of Sunday in other ways than in going to church. Preachers, we are told, are at a great disadvantage. They labor under a tremendous handicap. People have acquired a great love of nature. They have also acquired the means of gratifying it. Preachers who used to dread a rainy Sunday have come equally to dread a fair one. The people stay at home if they see in the heavens a cloud the size of a man's hand. But they flock to the shore or to the country if they behold the sun shining in the same heavens. The pace of modern industry and the multiplied demands on one's time make attractive a day which has no fixed engagements with God or man, and make it easy to resist the call of the church bell and to decline the effort required to get ready for church and to get there. And no effort is needed. The radio does it for them, without the intrusion of the contribution plate. The enormous amount of interesting and of profitable literature within easy reach, for the reading of which the other days of the week afford scant leisure, suggest other uses for Sunday morning than "going to church." And the decay of spiritual gifts has weakened both the desire and the capacity to share in the service, or to care for the sermon which the church provides. All of this and more is doubtless true. Yet in the face of it one may say that never in any age did the Christian preacher ever possess an opportunity so high, so great, as he possesses today.

For one thing, there has been a remarkable return in our day to religion as a dominant human interest. The fact is that all the sincere thinking of our time has broken through and beyond the barriers of a purely secular knowledge. Even the secular sciences, as they are called, carried to the extreme bounds of our modern knowledge, have ceased to be secular and have entered the mysterious domain of spiritual inquiry.

This theological mood, which may be said to underlie alike the best thinking and the best living of our day, has, by a curious process—in part the result of the post-war psychology—become the popular mood as well. All of a sudden, as it were, theology has become a popular interest. The theological controversies in which we find ourselves here in America at the present time, unhappy in some respects, at least have had the advantage that theology has, so to speak, been put back upon the map. Churches and halls are crowded today to hear theological debates. And after you have eliminated the curiosity-mongers and the scandal-hunters, you have left a multitude who are truly interested, whose sympathies are aroused, who feel keenly and vitally the importance of the issues that are involved. Every student of church history must have marveled at the serious way in which the Christian world took its theology in the old ante-Nicene days. Here were the people getting so excited over nice points in theological definition that they were excommunicating and banishing men right and left, and society was in an uproar. How unreal, how remote, that often seemed to us. But it does not seem unreal or remote any longer. Theology has once more become a storm center. The papers which with rare exceptions never thought of printing a sermon now publish religious news by the yard. And people have been reading and talking. They have been making up their minds. Some of these people doubtless have not examined their theological foundations for years. They have hardly known what they have believed, or why they have believed or if they have believed. But now the subject of theology is pushed to the front. Men are asking all kinds of questions. They are looking for guidance and light. Thus a great opportunity is presented to the preacher who knows how to meet it. And it ought to be met. But there is only one man who can meet it. The preacher who can minister to the chaotic theological unrest of our time will be one who is fully trained alike in secular culture and in the historic theological disciplines. He will know how to present ancient truth in modern language. Beyond this, however, there will be the evidence that for him theology is only the outward form and expression of an inward faith born of experience. Let men once discover that religious reality is behind all that he says, and they will welcome the interpretation of that experience in an orderly theology. There is an immense opportunity for such preaching in our modern world.

In addition, however, to this general emergence of the theological interest, the preacher finds many other encouragements to his spiritual witness. Preaching always comes to the front, is given its finest chance for influence, is allowed to climb to the heights, when the external conditions of life are disappointing, bewildering, and depressing. Rarely has the lamp of religion, for example, burned so feebly; rarely has morality sunk so low, as in the days of the eighteenth century, when the preaching of the Wesleys and of Whitefield startled the English-speaking world. That was a time for preaching to come into its own, and it did. A preaching that was born of God was given a glorious scope and power. It is on record that Whitefield preached to Yale students on one occasion with such effect that after the preaching, to use Whitefield's own words, "The President came to me as I was going off in the chaise and informed me that the students were so deeply impressed with the sermon that they . . . earnestly entreated me to give them one more quarter of an hour's exhortation." [7] Hard times in politics, in morals, in social conditions, have always been good times for religion. Such is the hour for which the Gospel was made, and in which the proclamation of the Gospel should be a joy and a spiritual triumph. Ministers of the Gospel in such days should hear a trumpet call that summons them to their task, and the tone of their utterance should give out no uncertain sound. Men are suffering in these days from mental and moral depression. Multitudes of thinking people have suffered moral and spiritual shell-shock. A mood of pessimism and of cynicism has replaced that of hope and faith. There is a weary feeling in many minds that life's problems are insoluble. We have had teachers declare that this is a blighted world and that human nature is bound to remain unaltered to the end. You can find this in much of the so-called best literature of the time, in poetry, or in the almost faultless English of Thomas Hardy's later novels. There are a hundred reasons for it. The over-devotion to the purely scientific method inevitably ends in a kind of intellectual disillusion. The worship, for

[7] Edward S. Ninde, *George Whitefield*, p. 147.

such it has amounted to, of the material world has produced a feeling of cynicism and left a void of empty regrets. The changed intellectual attitude has made many doubt and stumble. The absorption in secular tasks and the more general diffusion of wealth has caused many to forget the unseen and the eternal. Upon all this is now placed the terrible disillusionment which has followed the Great War. The prophets of pessimism and the voice of despair are abroad in the land. Bertrand Russell has been talking about the "doom, pitiless and sure," that will overtake the human race, when "the whole temple of man's achievement must inevitably be buried beneath the débris of a universe in ruins." [8] An American, Brooks Adams, has written a book entitled *The Degradation of the Democratic Dogma.* In it, he points out that the democratic idea has, so to speak, been the intellectual property of the Adams family from the very birth-hour of the Republic: with this difference, that John Adams and John Quincy Adams were convinced that at last the formula had been found which was to spell the salvation of mankind; whereas in our own day the Adams family is convinced that, like every other form of social experiment, it is headed for chaos. No wonder if people are inverting Browning's words, and are saying on every hand, "Is God in His Heaven, since Hell's in the world?"

Here, then, is a popular mood in which preaching ought to shine like a bright and burning light, and in which the proclamation of the everlasting Gospel should rise to its heights. The true preacher today will not linger on surface themes, nor will he make helpful deductions from "current events." Rather he will draw his inspirations from the deepest sources and proclaim a faith that

[8] *A Free Man's Worship,* quoted by Dean Inge in *Outspoken Essays,* Second Series, p. 168.

is rooted in the moral nature of God Himself. The Bible will be his inseparable companion, and the recovery of its message will be his most sacred task. For one of the most glowing and glorious characteristics of the Bible is its fundamental note of hopefulness. Dean Church of England once said that the Bible from beginning to end is one unbroken call to hope. Open the Bible anywhere and you will find hope glowing at the center of it. You can find plenty of evil in the Bible, and struggle, and defeat, but you cannot find despair. The heroes and the heroines of the Bible may be faulty in other respects: but every one of them is a matchless example of hope. The preacher in our modern world will reproduce the message of hope which underlies the Bible. He will make his own the triumphant mood of the Old Testament prophets who did not hesitate, upon the guarantees of God, to prophesy salvation for the people of God at the very hour when the national hopes were falling into ruin. He will deepen his faith in the omnipotence of the will of God whose word will not return unto Him void. He will recover the New Testament mood which was throughout one of unshakable serenity and confidence while the world itself was shaken as never before. And he will place his confidence where the New Testament writers placed theirs, on the immovable foundation of the Person and work of Jesus Christ. He will proclaim in the words of the aged Simeon: "This child is set for the rising and falling of many in Israel and for a sign that shall not be spoken against." [9] He will declare with Paul that "He must reign till He hath put all enemies under his feet." [10] With the eye of the author of the Epistle to the Hebrews, he will see "Jesus . . . crowned with glory and honor," even if "now we see not yet all things put under Him." [11] And the modern preacher will re-

[9] Luke ii. 34.   [10] I Cor. xv. 25.   [11] Heb. ii. 8, 9.

cover the accent of the author of the Apocalypse, who had indeed his own way of reading history; who read it as the unfolding of the will of God in the hands of the invincible Christ; who saw in all evil the impotent raging on earth of the serpent which already had been vanquished and cast out of heaven, which in a sure and fixed time was to be vanquished also on earth by Christ and His saints, and cast into the lake of brimstone and fire. He will preach in the faith of those magnificent words which stand over the chancel of Westminster Abbey: "The kingdoms of this world are become the kingdoms of our Lord and of His Christ, and He shall reign for ever and ever." [12]

Is there any question of the need of such preaching in our day? Is there any question of the value of it? "I've been to church," says Robert Louis Stevenson, "and I am not depressed." Consider the phrase and ponder its significance. You can turn it in one of two ways and you get your meaning either way. Did he mean that usually going to church depressed him? Then you have your meaning there. Did he mean that a man may be depressed before he goes to church, but that when he comes out of it he can be depressed no longer? Then you also get your meaning there. That is what the church ought to mean.

The greatest danger which threatens us today is that of moral and spiritual despair. A man needs to know, to use a beautiful phrase of Bishop Paget, that "there is that going forward in the world with which a man may link his labour without fear of spending it in vain." It is given to the Christian preacher today to offer to men that ultimate ground of assurance and hope. It is given to him to point men to Christ, the visible Incarnation of the invincible Love and Life of God. It is given to him

[12] Rev. xi. 15.

to remind men that this omnipotent Savior for His last word uttered the matchless promise: "I am with you always even to the consummation of the world." [13]

"Behold, I have set before thee an open door." [14] When in the whole history of the Christian church has it had an opportunity commensurate with the opportunity as it exists today? Look down for a moment into the coming years and imagine what it will mean if the world of our possessions becomes also the world of our faith; if the world of our knowledge becomes also the world of our hope; if the world of our power becomes the world of our love. Men everywhere are feeling that this is indeed a critical age, in which human destiny for untold generations is being fashioned either for weal or for woe. And men are turning and are looking to the saint and to the prophet who can utter the deep things of the Spirit; who can steady and guide the human soul as it seeks to find the path that leads to peace and salvation. Let one, in whose heart abides in rich measure the faith and the love that are in Christ Jesus, announce that faith clearly and rationally, and yet with the passion of personal conviction, and he will be satisfying the thirst of many souls. "O Timothy, that good thing which was committed unto thee keep by the Holy Ghost which dwelleth in us."

[13] Matt. xxviii. 20.   [14] Rev. iii. 8.

CHAPTER VII

THE CHRISTIAN EXPERIENCE AND THE CHRISTIAN PASTOR

THOMAS CHALMERS once said of Bishop Butler that he was "entirely void of the 'sal evangelicum.'" That is a fatal lack and loss. Without the evangelical salt and seasoning the Christian minister will have, as Chalmers asserted of Butler, a "meager and moderate theology," a "lax and superficial creed." Without it, preaching, however strong and brilliant in other respects, lacks the note of spiritual understanding and of spiritual authority which wins for it the response and acceptance of the human heart. In addition to all this, the *sal evangelicum* will be found to be the secret of the work of the Christian pastor. It is this which gives him the spiritual equipment, the native culture, the refinement and sensitiveness to spiritual realities, the sympathy and the passion which are the indispensable qualities of those who seek to be true shepherds of the souls of men.

The pastoral work of the Christian minister is one of the most delicate, the most difficult, the most important, and the most demanding vocations to which anyone can give himself. It has a technique that is all its own. This is painfully and carefully acquired. But when anyone has even to any degree mastered it there is opened up before him an endless spiritual opportunity, the joy, the satisfaction, the romance of which increases year after year. This ministry comes to monopolize more and more of his time and strength. It is so personal and obscure that no one knows or hears anything about it. Quiet pastoral duty done out of sight of the public promises nothing to the love either of sensation or of notoriety. It makes enormous demands upon spiritual resources as well as upon physical strength; and the ends it seeks and the rewards it gives are those which only a true lover of souls will value.

Pastoral work formed a large part of the ministry of Jesus. It is extraordinary how often those who seek to qualify as ministers of Jesus forget this. "Have you ever noticed," Henry Drummond once asked, "how much of Christ's life was spent in doing kind and helpful things—in merely doing kind and helpful things? Run over it with that in view, and you will find that He spent the greater portion of His time simply making people happy—in doing good turns to people." The greatest thing, someone has said, a man can do for his Heavenly Father, is to be kind to some of His children. It was this greatest thing that Jesus was always doing.

As we read the record of the pastoral work of Jesus, we are impressed with the extraordinary skill and insight with which this work was done, the nicety with which He met every problem of personal need. Sometimes He seems severe, but that severity when examined is seen to fit the moral need with entire exactness. At other times He seems extraordinarily broad and charitable in His judgments, yet how unerringly that charity comprehended the moral necessities of the case. Observing Him, we see the physician or the surgeon in a vast human clinic, fitting the moral remedy to the human need with a precision born of entire knowledge and with the authority of the Master.

It was as the apostles possessed and to the degree that they possessed and reproduced the mind of Christ that they continued this ministry to the needs of the individual life. When we read carefully the book of Acts and the

Epistles, we discover that behind all these missionary programs and journeys, all these matters of church organization and interest, there ran a beautiful and a life-giving stream of kindness, of loving ministry to individual men and women. These are the stories that ought to fasten our attention and interest. Peter and John were not so engrossed in their ecclesiastical problems that they did not notice the lame man at the beautiful gate of the Temple. Philip was not so preoccupied as he traveled in the desert that he failed to see the Ethiopian who was puzzling over the words of Isaiah. The missionary journeys of Paul would be dull reading if they were not enlivened and made human by stories of what he was forever doing for individuals. Read his letters and count the names of the many men and women whom he had learned to know, to love, and to help. Timothy himself is a kind of first fruit of his constant pastoral interest, and so were Eunice and Lois. To the end of his life this kind of ministry was a sort of passion with Paul. As a prisoner at Rome he made a captive for Jesus of the Roman soldier with whom he was handcuffed. We owe the beautiful little Epistle of Philemon to the fact that a poor runaway slave was not too lowly or obscure a child of God to escape the pastoral eye and heart of the great Apostle to the Gentiles.

Paul is very anxious that young Timothy should qualify as a good pastor. These epistles which bear Timothy's name are called the Pastoral Epistles. They have much to say about the details of the Christian ministry. But Paul knows well that underneath all else, if one is to be a good pastor, there must be an evangelical experience of the heart of Christ. So in charging his young disciple he admonishes him to keep warm within him by the Holy Ghost the faith and the love that were in Christ Jesus.

A ministry in Jesus' name will always magnify the pastoral office. It will resemble in this respect the ministry of Jesus Himself. Get within any really great ministry, and you will find that no matter how noble the sermons may be, no matter how large the ministry may bulk in the public eye, that man's days are crowded with numberless acts of kindness to individuals. He is repeating daily the ministry of the Good Shepherd.

The only way, however, to reproduce the ministry of Jesus is to share in the inspirations which underlay that ministry. This thing cannot be learned from the outside. It must issue from within. No man can make himself a good pastor by strenuous effort. Only God can make a good pastor. The pastoral instinct is one of the most beautiful fruits of a Christian experience of God. It comes naturally and unconsciously to the one who knows the love of God in Christ Jesus, our Lord. To minister as Jesus ministered, one must know the love of Jesus for men, and the faith of Jesus in men.

First of all, there must be the love. No one has a right to be a Christian minister whose supreme interest does not center in human beings. He may possess all other qualifications, but if he likes books or study, investigation or research, administration or organization, speaking or lecturing, more than he likes human beings, he will never make a successful minister of Jesus Christ. He ought to value books; he must continually and energetically study; he should have abilities as an organizer and administrator; but above all, beyond all and within all, he must have an absorbing interest in the lives and souls of men. This must be his supreme preoccupation. These are his specialty. When one elects to be a minister of Jesus, one deliberately chooses to spend one's time in dealing with individuals.

This love of men will be of no generalized sort. Paul used a great phrase once when he said, "The love of Christ constraineth me." The word "constrain" in this connection means to focus. There is a good deal of love in this world which does not focus. It is vague, abstract. It is a sort of benevolent sentiment for mankind in general. But for Paul, to know the love of Christ meant the opposite of all this. It caused him to concentrate his love on the concrete problems of individuals. The reality of all pastoral work can be tested in the same way. Moreover, it can be tested by the degree with which one gives one's self. No love does much which stops short of the giving of oneself. We do not really help men much when we give them money, nor when we give them an hour, nor when we give good advice or sound counsel. We help a little, but we do not help much. We do not help much until we give ourselves. And if we are to give ourselves there must be a self to give. And the only self, the giving of which can do much for any other self, is a self which has been quickened, inspired, reinforced by contact with, and by partaking of, the life of God Himself. It is the personality of Jesus alone which explains the ministry of Jesus. It is because He came forth from God that He entered as He did into the life of man. And it is in proportion as the minister of Jesus Christ shares, and to the degree that he shares, Jesus' experience of God that he will repeat the ministry of Jesus. For there is no balm in Gilead that can heal a wounded will, and there is no force in things that can lift a sunken life. It is only life which really touches life, and it is only soul which can touch and quicken another soul. All the difference between reality and sham separates a love which penetrates into the center of another's being because of the swift outgoing of oneself, and every lesser or more mechanical attempt at human helpfulness. John Galsworthy in his *Pigeon* contrasts what he calls the theorist philanthropist with the man who had a heart:

> If I had one prayer to make, it would be: "Good God, give me to understand." Those, sirs, with their theories, they can clean our skins and chain our habits; that soothes them for the aesthetic sense. It gives them, too, their good little importance. But our *spirits* they cannot touch, for they never understand. Without that, Monsieur, all is dry as the parched skin of an orange.

It is from that kind of second-rate, bogus pastoral work that every true minister of Jesus Christ should pray to be delivered. Read the life of William Booth, and you will discover what love means. It was the overmastering love of that man for poor struggling humanity that made him great. He loved the poor with a love that was the very breath of his life.

> Perfect love, we say, is not to be expected; and yet Christianity is either perfect love, or it ceases to be Christian. The Christian ideal, it is said, has not been tried and found wanting; it has been found difficult and left untried. Nevertheless, to read the Gospels in church, to pray for love, to preach about love, making not one single effort of love in our dealings with the abandoned or the lost, is not this manifestly to live our lives outside of the Kingdom of Heaven? [1]

No man on earth has such an opportunity for the most beautiful, constructive, and romantic form of personal influence as a Christian minister. But he can know it and wield it only as he knows in the most vital way the secret and the passion of Christ's love for men. It

[1] Harold Begbie, *Life of William Booth*, Vol. II, p. 442.

was Lyman Abbott, I believe, who pointed out how perfectly Paul, in his immortal chapter, described this love of Christ for men:

> Jesus suffered long and was kind; Jesus envied not; Jesus vaunted not Himself, was not puffed up. Jesus did not behave Himself unseemly, sought not His own; was not easily provoked; thought no evil. Jesus rejoiced not in iniquity, but rejoiced in the truth. Jesus bore all things, believed all things, endured all things. Jesus never failed.

And to the degree that we love men as Jesus loved them, we shall not fail either.

To the love of Jesus for men, we will add, however, Jesus' faith in men. He knew that every man was born of God. And it was to the godlike which He saw in every man that He made His appeal. "He knew what was in man." He knew that in every human being there lies the spark of immortal beauty to be fanned into flame by one rightly directed breath. His eye constantly pierced beneath the surface and found pure gold where to other eyes there was nothing but dross. He saw real value in the bruised reeds of human wills and in the smoking flax of human hearts. "There could be no grain of gold in any life that He did not see it and love it; there could not be the slightest tremble of good in any soul of all the multitudes before Him that did not touch His life and make it tremble too." And what we call the miracles of Jesus in dealing with men were performed by having faith in them and thus causing them for the first time to begin to have faith in themselves. He believed in men, in their capacity for moral self-recovery, and so He made them believe in the possibility of that self-recovery. It was the divine strategy of Jesus in dealing with men, and it never failed. He saw a man where others saw only a blind man or a leper or a lunatic. And it was to the manhood in the man that Jesus made His appeal, that manhood which in spite of all degradation had not lost all semblance to the image of God. He had a perfect faith in the infinite possibilities of every last child of God. He would take a beggar or an outcast and He would point him to the skies. He saved men because He believed that they could be saved, and so they were saved. He had great expectations of what men might become, and so they became according to His expectations. There is no helping men short of sharing in Christ's infinite faith in men. It is easy, perilously easy, for a Christian minister, unless he shares daily in the wealth and depth of the Christian experience, to fall into cynical, critical, secular judgments of personality. Unless we preserve Jesus' faith in man we are likely to make police-court estimates of them, to make what are called common-sense valuations of people. But Jesus never made a common-sense estimate of a man. He made an uncommon-sense estimate of him. He never used rough proverbs about people. He never said, "You cannot make a silken purse out of a sow's ear." Rather in the most hopeless and abject of human beings He saw a pearl of great price to redeem which He sold all that He had that He might make it shine like a jewel in the diadem of God. All great saving ministries have that faith enshrined within them. It is one of the most glorious characteristics of the Salvation Army. It shares Jesus' faith in men, and it gets great results out of broken bits of humanity. It is the indomitable conviction of its workers that by the grace of God man, any man, can be what he ought to be. To be a Christian pastor it is necessary to possess in large measure this unshakable faith in men. Only so can we go as Christ went, to the ruined and desolated, to the despairing and the bewildered among men, with the song of the day that is to be, and of the grandeur of a restored and recovered character.

Thus equipped with the love for men and the faith in men that were in Christ Jesus, the modern minister will enter, as Jesus entered, the arena of life, filled with its personal problems, its distorted beliefs, its disordered conduct, its morbidities, its dislocated relationships, its perplexities and abnormalities, and there see opened out before him a career of extraordinary interest and influence. As it unfolds before him, it becomes the dominating interest of his life. It never loses its fascination. One of the constant and beautiful surprises of his life is the way in which people from whom apparently little was to be expected surpass those from whom he had expected much. As he trusts men, as he is patient with them, above all, as he loves them and has faith in them, he has the richest rewards that can come to any man. He gets results of the most visible kind; he sees things done which are, of all things, perhaps, most worth the doing.

In proportion as he has an evangelical experience of the heart and life of Jesus, his ministry will begin to reproduce the exquisite qualities of the ministry of Jesus. For such a one, what is called pastoral work is redeemed from tedium, from routine, from dreariness. Without doubt, that is all that pastoral work means for many men. It is simply so much time lost from other and more important activities. A parish is rated high which does not "expect much pastoral visitation." But all of this way of measuring one's ministry is to invert the real method of Jesus. This was precisely the way in which He spent the most of His time. And that also was the way in which He won His greatest earthly joy. If there was joy in heaven over one sinner that repented, there was the same joy in the heart of Jesus. To spend our time and to spend ourselves as Jesus spent His time and spent Himself is to enter into that joy. Once let any humble minister of Jesus Christ share His love for men and His faith in men, and what is loosely and carelessly spoken of as pastoral work becomes the most romantic and the most alluring part of his life. Then he understands the significance, the pathos, the appeal of the great mass of inarticulate and uninterpreted experience which his parish represents. Then he has no higher ambition than to qualify as an interpreter of this experience. He understands that his function is to supply the missing word, to uncover the meaning of the deep human revolt from sin, to steady faith's wavering hand until it rests in the clasp of the Christ whom it dumbly seeks, to disentangle all kinds of involved personal situations and relationships, to help unveil the God for whose face men are evermore asking. To be able to enter into this world of inner experience and to acquire the ability to touch the springs of faith and action, and in the name of Christ to do the work of Christ, this is the highest privilege he knows. Pastoral work yields him a constant, uninterrupted joy—a joy more subtle, more exquisite, more delicate than comes to him in any other way. No work in life appears so fascinating as this. He looks forward with unspeakable gratitude to this kind of service, day after day, and year by year. He knows nothing of the restlessness, the longing for place, promotion, or the outer signs of professional progress. Every year will find him eager to take up his work where he left off. This is no ideal picture. It is an actual description of the profound satisfaction which thousands of humble shepherds are finding in pastoral work. The smallest parish furnishes all the opportunity which they desire. Not long ago a man died in the early years of his ministry.

In speaking of him an older man used these words: "He was a true parish priest. As my assistant, he had charge of a little mission district. He fell in love with it. He did the finest and highest quality of work there. He was absolutely contented in his little parish. At least, I had to make him leave it. Left to himself, he would have spent his life there." When once one has discovered the unending satisfaction in this kind of pastoral experience, nothing can take its place.

It is humble work. No one hears about it. It is not like making a great address and getting one's name in the papers. It is hard work. It takes all that there is of one. It took all that there was of Jesus. We are astonished when we read the record by the outpouring of divine love and life and feeling upon solitary and inconspicuous lives. As Horace Bushnell once said, "the expense of the sacrifice wears a look of extravagance." If men were the dull mediocrities which they are commonly taken to be, it would be quite inexplicable. But if Jesus, seeing through their possibilities into their real eternities, comprehends in the view all that they are to be and become as powers of an endless life, then this justifies all the concern He testifies, all the sacrifice which He makes. It is only as the souls of men committed to our care grow dull and lusterless before our eyes that we begrudge them the full giving of ourselves. It is only as we see them with the eyes of Jesus that no sacrifice is too great for one of the least of these. It takes a great deal of trouble and thought and time and self-sacrifice to know people, to say nothing of helping them. But if it were worth Christ's thought and life, surely it is worth ours. And after all, what is there in the world besides people?

If a minister's greatest joy lies in the sphere of his

pastoral service, there is where his greatest possible influence lies also. All around us men are talking of the place and worth of the church to modern society. The value of many of its forms of activity is frankly questioned. Its chief reliance upon preaching has been openly called a mistake. But if every minister of Jesus Christ would only faintly reproduce the ministry of Jesus to individuals, no one would question its worth. The recovery of this form of personal ministry upon the part of the rank and file of Christian ministers would go further perhaps than any other form of endeavor to rehabilitate the church in the mind and affection of our modern world. Such a preacher as Reginald J. Campbell has written that he considers the side of his ministry which has had to do with the care of individuals to be as fruitful as any; that he has done as much in this way as from the pulpit.[2]

> I see now the value of the confessional as an institution. . . . There is that in human nature which finds relief in uttering to human ears that which must ordinarily be kept between the soul and God. The mere act of telling is a help, and if this craving were to find no outlet, there would be many thousands of our fellow-creatures condemned to bear in secret a burden which grows heavier with the years. The longing for the word of authority, the word of comfort and release, from the lips of God's minister is a longing which cannot be ignored and ought not to be denied. Sickening abnormalities came my way—little of this personal dealing with souls had a definitely theological bearing. It was pathological rather than theological. I look back with profound humility and enhanced respect for poor struggling, aspiring humanity. If we knew more, we would censure less.

[2] *A Spiritual Pilgrimage*, pp. 157-161.

The point is, that the same kind of morbidity, of abnormality, confronts every minister of Jesus Christ. And if he begins to qualify as a priest to whom men are glad to confess, he does more good, perhaps, than in any other way. It is wonderful how few people there are to whom we can open our minds freely; how few to whom we would dare to humiliate ourselves by admission of weakness and failure; how few to listen and to understand. The sinner is well advised in shielding his soul when possible not only from the unfriendly scrutiny of his fellow-sinners, but from that scrutiny which is not intentionally uncharitable. Yet there is the need. The remorseful erring one wants to bare his heart; wants to hear human lips pronounce in God's name the good tidings of pardon and peace; wants direction, encouragement, moral guidance. Let a minister of Jesus Christ qualify as one to whom others are glad to confess, as one capable of performing this hidden and delicate service for the souls of men, and there is no arithmetic which can compute the value of his work.

Moreover it is such work which makes real preaching possible. People want good preaching. But how can a man preach effectively to people whom he does not know? How can he bring the Gospel he is commissioned to declare to bear upon experiences he knows nothing whatever about? It is an ignorant notion that parish visitation takes the time which ought to be devoted to sermon-writing. The most helpful preachers are always the best pastors. Of course, a man can be foolish in the way he orders his time. He can scatter his hours about in a reckless way that will leave him scant time for reading, study, and meditation. He can and he ought to keep morning hours to himself, and give the rest of the day to faithful pastoral ministration. No one who has traveled in Palestine can ever make the pernicious distinction between preaching and pastoral work. He sees the feeding of the flock by the shepherd just as Jesus saw it. He observes that many of the sheep will come up and eat at feeding time what is placed before them. But he observes also that many, if they eat at all, must be fed from hand to mouth. No preacher who contents himself with the wholesale feeding of the congregation once or twice a week can ever qualify as a good shepherd of Jesus Christ.

Once more, it is by this quiet, faithful pastoral service that a Christian minister acquires the confidence and devotion of his congregation, that spiritual basis upon which all the success of his ministry may be said to depend. Though a man speak with the voice of an archangel and hath not love, it profits him nothing. But let him possess "that good thing" in abundant measure; let him be a truly humble man who has gone down deep into himself and abides there and walks with God there, and so becomes the revered pastor and healer of the souls of men, and verily he has his reward. Quietly and steadily, as he goes on loving his congregation and giving himself to them, those invisible bonds will form on which his ministry will safely repose. A minister does not win the confidence of his people by preaching a great sermon. He does win it by being himself daily and hourly a living illustration of the Gospel which he preaches. "That man was made to be loved," Edmund Burke once said of Charles Fox. One who knew Henry Drummond declared that in him was to be seen the most beautiful exhibition of God's Spirit that he had ever witnessed. There never was a minister of Jesus Christ more loved than Phillips Brooks. Every mail brought him some word of homage from some friendly and grateful heart. Why this homage? It was because of his excellence as a human being, because of his pure goodness, because of his universal sympathy, his unrestricted compassion. It was because he loved himself last. Or take Thomas Chalmers. Before he died he was venerated from one end of Scotland to the other, by high and by humble, by all sorts of human beings. For a decade before he died he had passed beyond the sphere of criticism into that of universal homage. Yet he seemed unconscious of it and went on his way, as Carlyle said, with "his heavenly industries," never giving a thought to the chorus of praises sounding round him every day. He was recognized as a universal benediction. He became this by the simple and mighty fact of his human excellence. Love never faileth. In many ways Dr. Alexander Whyte may be said to have been the spiritual successor of Thomas Chalmers. By general consent of the Scotch he was the foremost saint, scholar, and preacher of his generation. He was loved by more people than any other man in Scotland. If we get at the heart of that ministry, also, we find that the secret of it was an evangelical and pastoral passion.

> Nothing [he wrote] will make up for a bad pastorate. The blood of Christ does not speak peace to my conscience in respect of a bad pastorate. Set every invitation and opportunity aside in the interest of a good conscience towards the homes of your people.[3]

And he set the example of just that thing. He knew all his homes amazingly well. He visited his parish systematically to the very end of his long ministry. He thought that it is what is going on in the insides of people that really matters. He would spend from two to three hours for five days in the week among the sick and lonely members of his congregation. Before each

[3] *Life of Alexander Whyte*, p. 528.

Communion Sunday he would send out post cards written with his own hand to the sick members of his flock, giving the full order of service, the Bible readings, the sermon subject. He held cottage prayer meetings. He endeavored to be present and conduct family worship on Sunday evenings in every home where death had entered the previous week. He was never too engaged himself to listen, with a smile which gave one the completest confidence, to all the perplexities which were brought to him. His presence itself was an inspiration. But it was his humility which most moved men. He gave one the distinct impression that he daily walked with God. No wonder such a man was loved and revered. True pastoral work always yields that rich and permanent reward. Let the humblest minister of Jesus Christ keep safe and warm in his heart that good treasure, the faith and love of Jesus Christ, and it will color his whole character. People will do more than "admire his sermons"; they will love the man. Little by little he too will pass beyond the sphere of criticism. He will acquire the authority of a pure, humble, and devoted minister of Jesus Christ.

Thus the cure of souls is the greatest of all callings, and it needs to be exercised with all the gifts that nature can bestow, all the knowledge of moral and mental problems that training can give, and the authority to give absolution to penitent men. Christian ministers need to be educated in many directions, but in none perhaps more than in this training to meet the problems of spiritual life.

Theological seminaries are giving increasing attention to this form of training, yet no outward or secular preparation will take the place of a deep inward and evangelical experience of the heart of Christ. In the long run, it will be found that nothing else, nothing less than this, will fit a man to do the deepest and best kind of pastoral work. This experience alone will give one, for one thing, that native inward refinement and sensitiveness, that spiritual quality, that insight and imagination, which are necessary to all such dealing with individuals. Spiritual quality, as we all know, is a difficult thing to describe. What is spiritual quality? Well, it is not piety in the common sense of that term: it is not necessarily religiousness; but, though it may be consistent with any religion, I do not see how it can be consistent with none. Spiritual quality: what can we call it but the "grasp of a Life, the knowledge of which is revealed to some babes and denied to some learned; which comes more by conduct than by study, and more by the grace of God than by either. Able men lacking it or losing this quality cease to be able to inspire leadership, and simple, unnoticed men and women possessing it are literally the salt of the earth." We have all known men and women who have possessed this gift of spiritual quality, these rich founts of inward resource, this rebound, these kindling qualities of life. Such a gift is the indispensable possession of any who seek to touch life with precision and with power. In the last analysis, it is the personality that cures. It is the man who gives the impression of being alive to his finger-tips, of not having a single torpid nerve in him, of possessing and communicating a life that comes from above and from beyond, the impact of whose personality is direct, vivid, authoritative—it is such an one who can exercise a spiritual ministry to individual men. In a word, he must have had his own "powerful, exquisite and delicate feeling for God." He must have had his own experience of God in Christ, his own blessed baptism of the Holy Ghost. Without this one may be admirably equipped for other forms of service; but both the will and the ability to serve people individually will be lacking.

Akin to this vividness of personality there will go another subtle but priceless gift: a certain refinement, reverence, sensitiveness, which lies at the heart of personal influence at its best. It is hard to find a name for this quality. Culture, perhaps, comes as near to it as any. But by culture we are now thinking not of an affair of the schools, but of the heart. The New Testament calls it "grace." When it speaks of the grace of the Lord Jesus Christ its chief meaning, without doubt, is loving-kindness and favor. But there is another meaning which also belongs to the word. The original meaning of the word "grace" as it is used in all Greek writers before the New Testament was written, a meaning which is perfectly familiar to all of us, was sweetness, charm, loveliness—a quality of life and of character that is distinguished by reason of great beauty. And however much the sense of the word might be deepened, it could never quite lose its original meaning.[4] When, therefore, the apostle prays that the grace of our Lord Jesus Christ might be upon his disciples, at least one petition within that great inclusive prayer is that the loveliness, the beauty, the personal attractiveness of Christ might become their spiritual property. The benediction contains the beautiful assurance that, if one has an evangelical experience of the heart of Christ, the beauty of the Lord will be upon him.

A great deal of the secret of the influence of Jesus lay in the fact that He was, one may say it in all rev-

---

[4] The word is used in this sense in the New Testament always, singularly enough, in relation to speech. When Jesus preached at Nazareth we are told that the people marveled at the words of grace, or gracious words, that proceeded out of his mouth. "Let your speech be always with grace," says the Apostle, "that ye may know how ye ought to answer every man" (Luke iv. 22; Col. iv. 6).

erence, the first of gentlemen. There was an indefinable delicacy, a tender and exquisite courtesy, in his dealings with men. There was an innate refinement which can better be felt than it can be described. It impressed men then, and it impresses us today. It was one of His spiritual qualities, a part of that spiritual equipment which enabled Him to impress and influence the lives of men.

Here is something that is often forgotten. Yet as a matter of fact the absence of just this quality of innate spiritual refinement prevents many ministers from qualifying as pastors. A young woman was once asked if she did not wish to meet the preacher whose church she was regularly attending. She declined the invitation on the ground that she feared that a more personal contact would destroy the impression produced by the service. Walk down the length of that sentence, and ask yourself squarely what lay behind it. People are much more delicately constituted than we often imagine, and the vague impression produced by one's very appearance and deportment has an immense amount to do with the confidence that he can win and the consequent influence that he can exert. It is strange, if we stop to consider it, what an impression, either helpful or otherwise, one's appearance and manner produces, entirely independent of anything that one says or does. One can feel that impression, but one can hardly analyze it. Yet the comfort or discomfort caused by the very presence and appearance of a person is far greater than we often think.

Mrs. Wharton in her novel *The House of Mirth,* uses a phrase to describe this very sensation. After Lily Bart had fallen out of her own world and was living with people beneath her in refinement and culture, she receives a visit from her old friend Selden. And she experiences an indefinable comfort just in being with him. "It rested her," Mrs. Wharton says, "the way he wore his clothes." I think we can feel the meaning of that phrase. There is a restfulness about what we call gentlemanliness. There is an impression produced by carriage and by manner that goes farther than we know. It is "the little touch of the superfluous which is necessary."

Thus the real pastor will have care to his appearance, to his carriage, to his speech. He will avoid every jarring thing, anything which can possibly offend the most sensitive taste. He will never indulge in anything which faintly approaches the coarse or the vulgar. It is not enough, Dr. Maltbie Babcock, that gallant and knightly soul, once said, that a minister's lips and hands should be clean. They must also be antiseptic. A minister who has regard for his spiritual influence will not make Bible jokes or speak in jocular fashion about his work or his sermons. Above all, he will refrain from funeral stories. These are a ministerial crime, a disgrace, and a scandal. There is no more sacred office which a minister of Jesus Christ is called upon to perform than to stand in the chamber and in the presence of death. It is a sacrament which for him should be covered with the most delicate reserve and the most austere silence. If you hear a Christian minister under any circumstances using a death scene to make people laugh, you have a right to conclude at once that he lacks one essential element of a true minister to the souls of men. Any word not conforming to the strictest canons of taste should be banished once and forever from the lips of one who aspires to be a helper to his fellow-men.

The question is, where is this innate and instinctive refinement to come from? Can it be acquired and how? It has been said that it takes three generations to produce a gentleman. Manner, at any rate, is a spiritual product.   Politeness, it has been remarked, involves a complete mastery of the Golden Rule.   I think one may go farther and assert that true courtesy involves the essential reverence of faith.   The essence of Jesus' profound respect and reverence for the human soul must lie within it and behind it.   It is this, and this alone, which can produce that type of character which has well been called a "spiritual gentleman," of whom a portrait has lately been given us: "the contagious quality of whose spirit was associated in the minds of many with the highest truths and the most beautiful qualities of the Christian spirit. . . . In his silences, in his speech, *the man he was* spoke with the authority of a great purity and with the eloquence of a lofty, sensitive and fine human spirit."   It is only the faith and love that are in Christ Jesus which succeeds in clothing "the great word 'gentleman' with spiritual significance and which gives to human character the tenderness and comforting power of Him in whom truth and courage and authority were at one with sweetness and refinement and with that imagination which takes all sorrow to itself and brings peace out of the fullness of a love to which no bitterness of experience is a stranger."

In the Epistle to the Hebrews the author has much to say of Jesus as the great high priest.   And it is to the minister in the rôle of priest that we ought to give increasing attention.   We think of him as prophet, and we think of him as manager, but we have thought about him too little as priest.   The word still sounds a bit strange in our Protestant ears.   Yet I have a feeling that it is only as we recover it that we shall also recover the thing for which it stands.   The word itself, of course, is only a variant of the word presbyter.   It stands for one who is older in his experience of God.   Thus understood the priesthood is the most venerable thing in the history of religion. Back of every document, every monument, every other witness to the religious life in men, there stands the shadowy figure of the priest "without father, without mother, without descent, having neither beginning of days nor end of life." [5] And if the priesthood is the most ancient of institutions, it is also the most modern. Everyone must have his priest. He must have someone to whom he can go in any hour of need; who, he believes, can speak to him with authority because of his own direct experience of God. A political ward boss was once asked how often he would "go to the front" for a follower who had been detected in crime. After he had said "yes" in response to the question if he would go once or twice, and the question was still pressed upon him, he replied, "Oh, go away; there has got to be someone in every ward that any fellow can go to whenever he needs help, hasn't there?" A pastor may well ask himself the question if in this sense he is the "boss" in his own parish. It is the only sense in which he should aspire to be. Is he the one to whom anyone will feel free to go whenever he needs help? Daily men and women are making confessions all around us to their own self-chosen priests. No outward authentication of this external priesthood is necessary. Henry Drummond never was ordained. But he heard more confessions than any man of his generation. Many men have been ordained, but because men do not see and do not feel in them the presence and the beauty and the power of the life of God, they may listen to their words, they may follow their directions as the leader of their parish, but they never think of telling them the inmost secrets of their hearts. No greater ambition should possess us than to be real priests to our people. We may succeed in all else, but

[5] Heb. vii. 3.

if we make a failure here we have fallen far below the possible level of our calling.

From this point of view a careful study of the Epistle to the Hebrews will show one the qualities which one must possess who cherishes the high and holy ambition to be a priest of God to his people. What were the qualities which made Jesus the perfect priest, according to this inspired writer? They were first, His perfect authority; and next His perfect sympathy. On the one hand He is "passed into the heavens," [6] but on the other hand "He can have compassion on the ignorant and on them that are out of the way; for that he himself also is compassed with infirmity." [7] These two qualities of authority and sympathy are indispensable to anyone who seeks to exercise the sacred office of the priesthood.

Of the one we have already spoken. The authority of the true priest, like that of Jesus, will not come from outward lineage or descent; it will be the authority of the Life that he possesses and of the Life that he is able to transmit. It will be the authority of a man who conveys the indelible impression that he has walked with God, that he knows by personal experience the things of God, and that he can pronounce with authority a message from God. Without the possession of this spiritual authority no man can qualify as a priest of the Most High.

But with authority there must be joined the quality of a true sympathy. I do not think that we yet understand what sympathy means. I think we should be driven back to the Gospels to study what real sympathy is. The great Englishman Bacon has a word to the effect that "the nobler a soul is, the more compassion it hath." Similarly, Lessing in his *Laocoön* puts pity as the divinest emotion of the human heart. From this point of view

[6] Heb. iv. 14.   [7] Heb. v. 2.

consider some characteristics of the sympathy of Jesus.

One is its intensity. When it is said that Jesus was moved with compassion, the verb is formed from the noun which means bowels. We are familiar with the expression "bowels of compassion." It is an easily discoverable fact that great mental emotions have a corresponding effect upon our physical organs. We all know what it is to feel sick at bad news. There is a sympathetic sensation caused by the deepest kinds of mental pain. It is this which is constantly ascribed to our Lord—a deep disturbing pain which could be felt as something physical. It is in this sense that it is said of Jesus that He was moved with compassion. It was not only the emergencies of life that called forth this pity. Life itself seemed to Him to be infinitely pathetic. He was intensely moved by the presence of any vast concourse or crowd of people. The very sight of a multitude was sufficient to call up His compassion. The very presence of a crowd of people had a peculiar and psychic effect upon His sensitive soul. "But when he saw the multitudes he was moved with compassion." [8] The very sea of upturned faces, the inward perception of how much moral destitution and unsatisfied spiritual aspiration, how much trouble, conscious or unconscious, was massed there, moved Him.

Another element in the compassion of Jesus was its continuousness. It was something that never wore off; its edge was never dulled. Constant contact with suffering did not blur the effect that it had upon Him. He never became so accustomed to it that He could confront it in concrete cases and not instantly react to it. He never got used to physical suffering. He never adopted that corollary, so attractive to some spiritual enthusiasts, that bodily suffering does not matter in comparison. It

[8] Matt. ix. 36.

always mattered to Him. He never became accustomed to human sorrow. The spectacle of it always moved Him. It might be the anxiety of a father for his son, of a woman for her daughter, of a master for his servant, but these appeals never became commonplace. Familiarity with suffering did not breed contempt for it. Quite the contrary; the more He saw of it, the more sensitive to it He became. It was a tireless continuing love, a permanent and dominant spiritual passion that ordered and controlled His life. "He loved them unto the end." [9]

Or note, once more, the personalness of Jesus' sympathy. It was called forth by and it was directed to concrete cases of suffering and need. When Jesus pitied, He pitied people. He pitied people with names. It was a certain man, a certain woman. One soul in need always stood in the foreground for Jesus. The story of the pity of Jesus is made up of concrete stories of individual men and women who called forth His pity, upon whom His compassion fell. We find no illustrations of it so vivid as those at the end of His life. Think of the stories of His compassion that crowd the record of His last journey to Jerusalem: He blesses the little children; He yearns over the rich young ruler; He heals the blind man near Jericho; He visits Zaccheus; He sups with Simon the leper; He blesses the woman who annointed Him with spikenard; and on the Cross itself He has words of pity and of welcome for the malefactor. An inspired artist carries the pity of Jesus even further. There is a moving canvas of the Descent from the Cross by Caracci which hangs in the Louvre. Before the body of Jesus there stands the figure of a little child. The arms of Jesus are seen enveloping and, as it were, protecting it. Even in death the love of Jesus seems unconsciously to go out to one of these little ones.

[9] John xiii. 1.

Finally, His compassion was constructive. It built up character. It made demands on faith. It called for performance. It developed manhood. It educated the will. To a paralytic who had lain so long beside the pool, without having anyone put him in, that more than his body—so that his will also—had become paralyzed, Jesus said, "Take up thy bed and walk." It seemed doubtless like an impossible commandment. It called for an exertion of the will that must have been tremendous. But Jesus always made demands upon the will. To the lepers who came for cleansing, He said, "Go, shew yourselves to the priests"; to the woman who was a sinner, "Go and sin no more"; to the man whose father had died, "Come, follow Me." The pity of Jesus was not weakening in its effects. It made strength, fibre; it tautened the will; it geared up and put into operation moral and spiritual resources which men did not suspect they possessed. Those whom He pitied did not feel any soft enervating influence. They got something like an electric shock. They were lifted out of themselves. It was not a sick body only, but an infirm will, a defective morale, that was healed by the constructive compassion of Jesus.

Such was the pity of Jesus. It was intense; it was continuous; it was personal; it was constructive. If it is true that "the nobler a soul is, the more compassion it hath," how noble is the soul of Jesus! If it be true that pity is the divinest emotion of the heart, how divine is the heart of Jesus!

Such a pity is the indispensable possession of a minister of Jesus Christ who seeks to be a true parish priest. In some deep way he must learn the secret of this alert, ready, watchful, unsleeping, commanding compassion of Jesus. And the danger is that it will be lost. The danger is that daily familiarity with various kinds of need will blunt our sensibilities; that our sympathies will become shop-worn; that our sensitiveness will gradually have the fine edge worn off of it. We will become so interested in the great appeals that come to us that we will overlook the little personal ones. That is the danger to which all parish ministers are exposed. The danger is that we will become so immersed in the technicalities of parish administration as to overlook the inarticulate human maladies with which every parish, even the smallest, is filled, waiting for someone to interpret them, and with delicate understanding to treat them and heal them. To keep sympathy keen, enduring, quick, discerning this is essential, if a minister is to do his best work in the daily cure of souls. The question is, how can it be done? How is one to have a compassion such as this become the increasing, deepening, and developing experience of his life? Someone has said that "to look upon the woes of men is sufficient to stir our pity in the extreme." But that simply is not true. We look daily upon the woes of men. Yet how really seldom is our pity deeply and effectively stirred, stirred to instant and self-sacrificing action? Even our passion for social service will not suffice. The trouble with our sympathies is that they are intermittent. They are roused for a brief moment by some extraordinary circumstance; when the emergency has gone, the compassion has gone also. It comes from the surface and not from the depths. It is manufactured from without; it does not well up from within. It is an affair of the moment and not the fine, sure, permanent quality of the soul. Our compassion must come from within if it is to become the habit, the instinct, the permanent passion of our lives. It has always been so with men who have known the meaning of compassion. *"La vie est une comédie à ceux qui pensent, une tragédie à ceux qui sentent."* The pitying love of

God in Christ has robed them. It has enveloped them. It has become an instinct with them. Elemental pity of this nature drains spiritual resources to the utmost. But no other kind of sympathy is good for much if it is good for anything at all. When Jesus' sympathy had done its work, He knew that virtue had gone out of Him. The healing of an anonymous invalid had taken toll of Him. And if our sympathy does any work, we will know it too.

For the final mark of the character of a true pastor is passion. He is a lavish spender of life. He knows little about economizing strength or resources. "I know how physicians lift wise voices against the 'pace that kills.' Meantime I observe that those physicians whose names are like ointment poured forth seem least regardful of the value of their own advice." [10]   It is said that ministers and farmers are the longest-lived members of the community. I have always backed away from that sentence. I do not know if ministers ought to live so long. Possibly some of us live too long. At thirty-one Moffatt got the answer to his prayer that he might "burn out for God." If we live long because we respect our bodies, observe the laws of health, live regularly, and know the meaning of self-control, that is one thing. But the poorest compliment ever paid a minister of Jesus Christ is to say that his task sits lightly on his shoulders. It was said of Abraham Lincoln that his face was a sort of map on which the battles of the Civil War were printed. And if a minister of Jesus Christ knows anything of the battles of Jesus, it must show in his face. Must we ministers learn what passion means from our laymen? No vast enterprise runs automatically. Its blood is always human blood. The brains of it are somebody's.

[10] George Clark Peck, art. in the *Christian World Pulpit*, February 7, 1917.

Somebody always pays the price. And if there is no frugal way to run a great business, least of all is there any economical way of doing the business of Jesus Christ. Of whom else shall it be so true as of the Christian minister?

> Measure thy life by loss instead of gain:
> Not by wine drunk but by the wine poured forth;
> For life's strength standeth in its sacrifice,
> And whoso gives the most hath most to give.

Yet such a decline in idealism, such a loss of original enthusiasm, is a moral peril in the path of everyone who enters the ministry. There are all kinds of obstacles: the work will tend to degenerate into parish routine; the resistance of church officials will be a yoke grievous to be borne; the early glamour of one's task will wear off, and, except one's life be deeply rooted in the life of God, enthusiasm will wear away also. Nothing but the experience of God who was in Christ reconciling the world unto Himself will keep the flame of our passion burning bright in spite of all difficulties and in the midst of all dangers.

Such, then, are the qualities of a true pastor: the authority of a pure and holy life, and a sympathy and spiritual passion which increase as time goes on and light up every aspect of his life and work. Such qualities are a spiritual product. They can spring only from a deep inward experience of God. They must come from an evangelical experience of God in Jesus Christ. Therefore, "O Timothy, that good thing which was committed unto thee, keep by the Holy Ghost which dwelleth in us."

CHAPTER VIII

The Cultivation of the Christian Experience

In no department of the minister's work is the presence or the poverty of the Christian experience more clearly revealed than in his conduct of worship.[1] The unspiritual minister stands unmasked at the moment of prayer. The service presents a far more serious problem than the sermon. Ministers themselves recognize this. It is easier, they feel, to preach a good sermon than to put into active operation spiritual forces that unite the whole congregation in actual communion with God. On this point there can be no question. The essential thing in worship is to realize the presence of God. A minister can produce the sense of God in others only in proportion as he possesses it in himself.

The demand thus made upon our evangelical and Protestant ministry is a critical one. Religion belongs to the mysteries, and its essential principle is a belief in and reverence for things unseen. At the heart of all true religion is the sense of awe in the presence of the Invisible. Worship is essentially an act of faith in which the worshipping heart lays hold of spiritual realities without desiring or endeavoring to explain or to understand them.

The Protestant minister, aware of this, who seeks to create the atmosphere of spiritual reality, who feels the deep need of reviving the spirit of awe, of spiritual ex-

[1] For a full discussion of this subject, see the author's *The Christian Church in the Modern World*, Chapter VII.

pectancy, in a word, of making the act of worship a central fact in the Christian cultus, will need himself to possess in large measure that sacred and secret treasure, the Christian experience of God. Not only will he all too often find nothing to help him in the church building or in the attitude and temper of his congregation, but he must combat a long-standing and deep-seated Protestant tradition. As Dr. Dawson has helpfully written:

> Protestantism [historically defined] is organized protest. It began in a courageous protest against forms of religious mystery which had degenerated into superstitions, but in rooting up the tares it destroyed much true wheat. It set itself against all mystery in religion, all symbolism; instead of mystery, it gave us controversy, and instead of symbolism, syllogisms. After several centuries spent in driving out of the church holy mysteries, it is extremely difficult to reinstate them; yet he is but a poor student of history and a dull observer of human nature who is not aware that the heart of man does crave mystery in worship, and is not satisfied with a temple which is rather a meeting-house for men than a house of God and the vestibule of eternity.[2]

The church, in a word, which is to do its real work in our modern world, hungry for spiritual certainty and for a sense of the reality of the things that belong to God, must above all else minister to the hearts of men by communicating that experience of God in Christ which is its peculiar treasure. It must make more of silent communion with God. It must not rely solely on public exhortation. It must organize itself as a channel for the communication of Divine Grace, and not merely develop itself into a superb machine for the getting and dispens-

[2] William J. Dawson, art. in the *Century Magazine*, September, 1923.

ing of money and for forming all kinds of groups for helpful secular activities. It must set itself against all cheap and vulgar methods of success which do little more than bring together a casual and capricious "audience." It must reach and quicken the "delicate God-lonesome soul of man" with a sense of the reality and nearness of God. It must make men say, "God is in this place. This is none other than the house of God, and the gate of heaven." [3] The profoundest error into which any minister can fall is one into which today he is most likely to fall: the error of believing that any amount of organization can take the place of piety and devotion.

The mistake is often made of supposing that the way to recover the act of worship in our churches lies in the putting on of a "liturgical order" of service. But it is not primarily a question of outward form or order at all, although these matters properly understood and valued have their importance. But the notion that a minister by merely manipulating the form of service may produce the spirit of worship is one which ought to be dismissed at once. The spectacle of modern ministers putting on "liturgical programs" which often bewilder and irritate their congregations would be comical if it were not so infinitely pathetic. The thing simply cannot be done by a process so mechanical as this.

Neither can it be done by the substitution of written for free prayer. In his effort to escape from what he feels to be the impossible task of free pastoral prayer, many a minister today betakes himself to the use of prayers composed either by himself or by others. As between the two, I advise the latter. But as the exclusive practice of the minister, I advise neither. Of the infelici-

[3] Gen. xxvi. 17.

ties of free prayer it is unnecessary to speak. Even at its best it is often ineffective.

> My Anglican ears [Cyril Hepher has written] tuned to the Elizabethan music of the Prayer Book, are conscious of something discordant in Nonconformist prayer speech. Even the cultured and eloquent phrases of Mr. Campbell, and the unadorned simplicity of Dr. Horton leave me unmoved. It may be a confession of weakness, but it is a fact. The inevitably recurring phrases of Protestant piety, defensible enough, "Lord Thou knowest," and the like, punctuating the sentences; even the psychological contributions of the New Theologian, "Lord, we are met for the reaffirmation of our better selves," thrill me as little as the catalogue of titles of Our Lady in the Litany of Loretto.[4]

On the other hand, there is no denying that free prayer may have an effect on the worshipping heart of a congregation for which there is simply no substitute. Anyone who has ever experienced the sheer lifting of an entire congregation into the presence of God by the power of prayer understands this. It may not always happen. It may not often happen. But when it does there is something supernal in its effect. Such prayer is so tender and direct, so aglow with sympathy and insight, so intimate without being familiar, so haunting in pathos yet so victorious in faith, as of one who knows how to climb up onto the knees of God and talk with the simplicity of a child.

> Never [Henry Ward Beecher has written] in my study, . . . never on the street, in those chance inspirations which every one is subject to; never in any circumstances of life, is there anything so touching,

[4] *Fellowship of Silence*, pp. 45-47.

> as when I stand in ordinary good health before my
> congregation to pray for them.[5]

"In ordinary good health" must mean in good spiritual
health as well as in good physical condition. The preparation for this deepest service of all goes deep, far back
of the occasion itself; it is found in the self-discipline, the
spiritual cultivation, the real devotion of the personal
life. The source and secret of prevailing prayer is found
in a truly evangelical experience of God. It is found in
a soul that is saturated with Bible thought and Bible language. Ignorance of the Bible betrays itself infallibly at
the moment of prayer. True prayer is not the language
of the school, but of the heart. And to make heart-
language ours we must be familiar with it. One who
really aspires to lead the prayers of the people will thus
train himself by contact to the point of saturation with
historic and individual forms of devotion. For in the
oldest liturgies is found worship at a high estate. But
above all he will keep rich and warm within himself the
realities of the Christian experience of God which can
touch, quicken, and illumine all the varied experiences
and needs of men.

There is, therefore, for the Christian minister, from
any point of view of his ministry, no substitute for first-
hand experience of the spiritual life. Upon the depth and
breadth of his evangelical experience of God will depend
the reality and the efficiency of his ministry among men.
We need to lay to heart the words of old Richard Baxter:

> When your minds are in an holy frame, your people
> are likely to partake of it. Your prayers and praises
> and doctrine will be sweet and heavenly to them.
> They are likely to feel it when you have been much

[5] *Yale Lectures on Preaching*, Vol. II, p. 46.

with God. That which is on your hearts most, will be most in their ears. I confess, I must speak it by lamentable experience, that I publish to my flock the distempers of my soul. You cannot decline and neglect your duty, but others will be losers by it as well as yourselves. If we let our love decrease, and if we abate our holy care and watchfulness, it will soon appear in our doctrine. If the matter shew it not, the manner will; and our hearers are likely to fare the worse for it. Whereas, if we could abound in faith and love and zeal, how would they overflow to the refreshing of our congregations! Watch therefore, brethren, over your own hearts. Keep out lusts, and worldly inclinations; and keep up the life of faith and love. Be much at home, and be much with God. If it be not your daily serious business to study your own hearts, to subdue corruptions, and to "walk with God," all will go amiss with you. Above all, be much in secret prayer and meditation. There you must fetch the heavenly fire that must kindle your sacrifices.[6]

These are the days in which this truth needs to be brought sharply to the attention of all who are already in the professional ministry or who are thinking of entering it. The danger is that with other equipment for our task, we shall lose the possession of that innermost treasure which alone gives meaning and glory to all else that we do. The menace of professionalism confronts every worker in any department of life. There is always the danger that the soul will go out of it, that one will become a routine performer instead of an originator, an imitator instead of a spiritual leader. What we call imagination, divination, genius—in a word, a mind in touch with reality—always distinguishes the first-rate from the second-rate performer in any department of human activ-

[6] *The Reformed Pastor*, pp. 100-101.

ity. Eckhard's well-known phrase, *"Dies Funkelein ist Gott"* has universal application. Always it is the spark, the mystical contact of the soul with invisible reality which makes any man or any work of man truly godlike.

True of every other form of human activity, it is supremely true of the Christian ministry. A Christian minister above and beyond all else must be a man of God. And he must be a Man of God in a definite and a specialized sense. The designation could not be refused of any faithful, sincere, devout man.   But the Christian minister above and beyond all else must be a man with whom the Spirit of God has clothed itself. He is under immense inward pressure. Not only his voice but his whole personality·must be an organ of the God-consciousness. He must be sensitive to divine intimations. His must be the utterance of a God-inspired, God-saturated personality. He must be sensitive to every breath of God. By the very nature of his calling that is what he must be. Though he be all else, and be not this, it profiteth neither him nor anyone else anything. Let him cease to be a mystic and become a mechanician, and he may remain a parish organizer and a parish worker, but he has ceased to be a prophet of the Most High and a minister of the riches of God in Christ Jesus our Lord.

Yet precisely that is the grave danger that does confront us. Many ministers, some without knowing it, have ceased to be mystics and have become mechanics. The divine spark has simply ceased to glow. It has become overlaid with the multitudinous duties to which our Protestant churches as at present organized condemn their ministers. He finds himself embroiled in countless activities which withdraw his energy from the center and dissipate it. He must respond to the needs of his parish, preside over all kinds of gatherings, be able to speak out of hand on every imaginable subject; imitate all kinds of goodness, "run" this and that, represent his congregation in denominational assemblies, be a credit to his church in local public affairs, suffer all the social entanglements which his position involves. Here is the minimum requirement expected of the professional ministry. No wonder if under these conditions, the divine spark has been smothered. Worse than this, the perception of its indispensable importance has been smothered also. The professional ministry more and more takes on the aspects of a commercial enterprise.

> A man looking forward to success in the ministry sees himself in the office of a well-appointed parish house; a secretary is busy typing; assistants, directors of religious education, volunteer workers, come and go. The hum of voices of those engaged in organization activities can be heard from the parish rooms. A pile of elaborate reports indicates a growing concern. And in the center of it all sits our man of God who oversees, directs, informs and controls the whole business.

There is much talk of the failure of the Church in our day. Some of it is wise and well-meant. Much of it is neither. As a matter of fact, the church fails when the prophetic, the mystical, note is lacking in its ministry. And no lover of the church can blink the danger which under modern conditions thus threatens its influence and its very existence. It has even been denied that, under conditions which prevail today, a prophetic ministry is any longer possible. "It may be stated boldly and bluntly that it is no longer possible for a professional ministry to be a prophetic ministry."[7] If, in addition to the disabilities already enumerated, be added domestic cares and worries—the responsibility

[7] Edward Lewis: art. "The Professional Ministry," *Atlantic Monthly*, December, 1915.

tacitly placed upon the parish minister to keep up the interest and Sunday congregations so that the parish treasury shall be filled out of which his own salary is to be paid upon which the maintenance of his family depends—the whole thing seems to be impossible. By no method, it is asserted, can the prophetic gift be kept alive under such conditions. It is a contradiction in terms. The situation resolves itself into an absurdity.

The answer to all this is that the thing has been done, is being done, and thus can be done. All over the land, in humble parishes as well as in conspicuous city churches, may be found men who correspond upon strictest analysis with the Men of God of whom we read in Bible and in history. The Spirit of God has clothed itself with them. They betray in face, in voice, in attitude, and in every human contact that they have been with Jesus. Like their Master mingling with all sorts and conditions of men, there is a difference, an apartness, neither of dress nor any outward sign, but wholly of spiritual quality, which indicates that their dwelling place is with Christ in God. When they speak, men listen not because they utter any enticing words of wisdom, but because they do hear the accent as of another world. They are daily and literally God-inspired, God-saturated men. They are "vibrant instruments to the breath of God." In sheer literalness we can call them nothing else, nothing less.

Their churches are in part responsible for this. The church leaders are wise enough to understand that the one thing needful for their Man of God is, that the divine spark shall not be smothered. Consequently they see to it that the demands of the parish do not murder him. They take off of his shoulders and off of his mind many harassing details of parish life. They let him alone.

They give him large open spaces for privacy, meditation, and inward brooding. They understand that it is out of the depths that the treasures of God will be brought, and that their Man of God must be left to discover the vein for the silver and the place where gold may be found. Their Moses shall not be so enmeshed in a wilderness of routine that he cannot speak with the voice of God from Sinai; neither shall their Isaiah serve on so many committees that he shall have no word of confidence and hope to utter for a beleaguered Jerusalem.[8] If churches understood the sources of spiritual supply upon which their very existence depends, they would not allow these to be clogged up by the accumulations of petty and continuous detail.

But when this thing is done, when the prophetic note is still heard, you will find that the Christian minister himself understands that his very life and usefulness, his dignity, meaning and value to himself and to all others, depend upon keeping "that good thing," his first-hand experience of God, fresh and warm and deep within his own soul. He understands that no amount of hustling will make up for a poverty of inward experience, a

---

[8] This has been eloquently described by Bishop Quayle: "Man and God, these the preacher has by heart. What a blessed luggage they are! The folks for whom God died, and the God who died for folks. The wideness of the world of ground and sky is on such a man. He walks in radiancies like a perpetual dawn. He talks with God; and God talks with him. And when the preacher comes to a Sunday in his journey through the week, people ask him, 'Preacher-man, where were you and what saw you while the workdays were sweating at their toil?' And then of this preacher we may say reverently, 'He opened his mouth and taught them, saying,' and there will be another though lesser Sermon on the Mount. And the auditors sit and sob and shout under their breath; and say with their helped hearts, 'Preacher, saw you and heard you that? You were well employed. Go out and listen and look another week; but be very sure to come back and tell us what you heard and saw.' That will be preaching" (*The Pastor-Preacher*, pp. 370-371).

gradual lowering of the spiritual tone and quality of his life.[9] By strength and by struggle, he will hold away from his soul the tides of *things* that threaten to engulf him. Hence, the cultivation and the development of his own inward life takes first place in the ordering of his daily existence, and not the last. He understands that this one thing must be done, though much else be left undone.

A minister in earnest about the cultivation of his inward experience of God will be on his guard also against the tendency to rationalize and to theorize about everything in heaven and on earth. A minister can make no greater mistake than to imagine that his hearers must have everything explained to their entire intellectual satisfaction. Protestantism has done a vast service in affirming the right of private judgment—in asserting the liberty of the individual to test for himself the content of faith, and in refusing to accept dogma on the authority of an external ecclesiastical tribunal. But Protestantism makes a fatal error if it falls into the opposite extreme and assumes that religious realities belong in the same category with sensible phenomena. Yet, to judge from their mental habits, and from their methods and message, that is just what many so-called modernists do. They rationalize and they argue; they debate and they defend; they employ the vocabulary of science and the dialectic of philosophy—but they do not announce out of a deep, personal—and mystical experience of religion realities which, if they are to be known in any positive fashion, can be known not by an outward method, but by a process that is inward and spiritual. What we need in our pulpits is not less logic, it may be, but a great

[9] See W. R. Inge, *Personal Religion and the Life of Devotion,* p. 31.

deal more of a personal religion born of a mystical apprehension of spiritual truth. This does not mean that[10] thinking men are to give up religious realities as impossible to think about or to content themselves with a vague religiosity, an unreal sentimentalism. But it does mean that when all is said and done, in the whole process of laying hold of the life of God in the sense that this becomes our own personal and spiritual possession, intellect, or the mere understanding, is but a subordinate agent and must be kept so. What we need above all else is "the hearing ear" and the "understanding heart," by which we may receive the testimony which God bears in every heart to those great truths which the Bible reveals. "This and not logic is the way to grow in religious knowledge, to know that the truths of religion are not shadows but deep realities." Rationalism, Dean Inge has said plainly, has not much place in the life of faith except as "checking the exuberance of the religious imagination." There are those who will dissent from this statement, who will find much more place and use for the intellect than this in the "life of faith." But is there any question that the average Protestant ministry is over-intellectualized, not in the sense that it is over-educated—it can never be that—but that it tends to place exaggerated emphasis on the intellectual processes for the discovery of religious reality. We need to ponder the meaning of such a sentence as this by the English mystic John Smith, from his treatise, which it would be well for all of us to read, on "The True Way or Method of Attaining Divine Knowledge:

> Divinity is a Divine Life rather than a Divine Science, to be understood rather by spiritual sensation than by verbal description. That which enables us to

---

[10] See J. C. Shairp, *Culture and Religion*, pp. 116 ff., p. 127.

know and to understand aright the things of God, must be a living principle of holiness within us.[11]

A minister needs to be a many-sided man if he is to succeed in his supreme task of communicating to men an authentic experience of God. He must possess a thorough understanding of the modern scientific and philosophical concepts of the world in which we live. He must also be thoroughly grounded in the external and historical basis of the Christian faith. Now, most so-called modernist Protestant ministers, to my thinking, do have both of these fairly well in their grip and possession. Where they fall short is in a third direction, in the experimental side of religion. I see little danger that our liberal Protestant ministry will fall into the perils of fanaticism, but I do see signs that it will allow its teaching to degenerate into an arid, an uninspired rationalism. Our Protestant ministry needs few things more than it needs the recovery of the mystical attitude and temper.

It is time that we came to grips for a moment with this word mysticism. "No word in our language," Dean Inge has written, "not even 'socialism' has been employed more loosely than 'mysticism.' "[12] To some it means a vague kind of sentimentalism; for others an impossible kind of pietism; for still others occultism or even fanaticism. The word has been so much abused that Principal Garvie feels that it ought to be banished; that Christian thinking would be clearer if it were rid of the word "mysticism" altogether.[13]

[11] Quoted by W. R. Inge, in *Christian Mysticism*, p. 290.
[12] *Op. cit.*, p. 3.
[13] "It is most unfortunate that the spiritual in Christianity has been so often described as the mystical and that men have advocated mysticism when they were really pleading for spirituality" (A. C. Garvie, *Christian Certainty Amid the Modern Perplexity*, p. 177).

As we have already seen, however, the word has a clear, technical meaning. Mysticism in religion, is the art of finding God in oneself. It is the science of union with God. It is the attempt to realize the presence of the living God in the soul and in nature. The difference between the mystical and the usual Christian experience is in degree rather than kind. There can be no personal religious experience without a mystical element. Mysticism is simply religious experience in an intense form. The mystic makes it his life's aim to be transformed into the likeness of Him in whose image he was created. He loves to figure his path as a ladder reaching from earth to heaven which must be climbed step by step. He has named these steps. First, there is the purgative step by which the soul becomes cleansed from all wordly elements; then, the illuminative, in which it begins to catch some vision of God; finally the unitive, in which the state of perfect contemplation and the sense of final union with God has been attained.

Now it is only speaking the truth to say that the average Protestant minister today, so practical, so rational, finds himself in a strange and even in an eerie world when he enters into fellowship with the mystics. That is just why he should enter into that fellowship. We need desperately a counter-balance to the tyranny of the secular and intellectual elements of our ministerial life. We need enormously an enlargement of the contemplative and mystical areas of our everyday experience. The very fact that, when one takes up the life of the mystics and follows the steps of their experience, one finds oneself led far away from one's usual mental preoccupations, shows how profound has been the neglect of a side of our nature—and that the deepest—namely, that which is most likely to lead us into a true knowledge of God out of which our whole ministry takes its form and meaning. It needs to be remembered that mysticism has let loose upon earth a spiritual dynamic.[14] There has never yet been a great religious leader who was not in some sense a mystic. Again and again mystical feeling has invigorated Christian activities. "It has been the motive power of Christian progress, the fire from which has been kindled the passion for service and the rule of duty. The river of God is full of water when the springs of mystical communion overflow." Nothing will do modern ministers more good than to read into the lives of these mystics. We will find them desperately in earnest in their quest for God. We will find them ruthless in their treatment of anything in themselves which they feel stands between them and the object of their supreme desire: the sight and the knowledge of God. We will find them developing a method by which that vision of God may be won, a method which they follow and practice with such fidelity and with such success that the vision of God is won. " 'Mysticism,' " says Edward Caird, "is religion in its most concentrated and exclusive form; it is that attitude of the mind in which all other relations are swallowed up in the relation of the soul to God."[15]

For the serious student of religion to throw all this lightly aside, for the minister who desires to cultivate within him the deepest sources of the religious life to disregard all of this as belonging to the pathological by-products of Christianity, is to be terribly shortsighted. It is, moreover, to remain out of touch with some of the deepest currents of the religious life of our modern world. Most people are far more mystical than they are given credit for. Precisely because of the bewilderment in which the catastrophe of the Great War

[14] E. S. Waterhouse, *The Psychology of the Christian Life*, pp. 62-63.
[15] Quoted by W. R. Inge, in *Personal Religion and the Life of Devotion*, pp. 18-19.

has left men; because they are discontented with the
moral short-sightedness and obtuseness of politicians,
discontented also with that tyranny of material things
and the ultra-rationalism which they all too often find
in the churches, multitudes are looking with new sympathy and hope to the mystical approach to the realities
of religion. Always in the history of religion, when the
outward framework of things has seemed to give way,
and reliance upon a visible order has been shaken, the
soul of man has yearned for an immediate vision of God
and has craved a direct experience of His reality and
power. The appearance of apocalyptical prophecy in
the Old Testament, with its message of the salvation of
God's people in defiance of all outward circumstance,
coincides with the collapse of the Jewish State and of the
political aspirations of the people. The emergence of
the Greek and oriental mystery religions, with their doctrine of salvation by secret initiation, occurs when the
structure of the Roman Empire is threatened with disso-
lution. Similarly, in our day, thoughtful people increasingly skeptical of the permanence and authority of the
outward and visible, are seeking a religion of the spirit.
They are finding in a direct approach to God, in a mystical experience of His reality, of His presence, of His
power, an answer to the problems of existence, a way
out of the difficulties in which they feel themselves to be
involved.

A concrete illustration of this lies in the personality
and work of Frank Buchman with college and university
students. Harold Begbie has given an illuminating and
sympathetic account of this movement in his well-known
More Twice-Born Men. It deserves careful reading by
all who propose to minister to the spiritual needs of our
modern world. Underlying the whole story lies the sig-
nificant fact that many college-bred men and women,

bewildered by the intellectualism of the schools, and failing to find either in ecclesiasticism or in rationalism an authoritative religious experience, have sought and found this in a direct and mystical approach to God. Thousands of people in the modern world are crying out for just this experience. They are weary of a religion which cannot give them the power of contact with the Unseen. Consequently, the message which most directly ministers to the spiritual needs of this generation is the gospel of the spiritual life and of personal spiritual development, of prayer, of communion with God. The men and women of our generation do not hunger either for orthodoxy or for liberalism; either for fundamentalism or for modernism. But they do long for personal illumination, personal inspiration, and the immediate touch with the spiritual world. There are signs that an age of the Spirit and of interior religion is approaching. So may it be. To put it briefly, there is more mysticism in the modern world than the average church and the average ministry provides for. And it is our business to provide for it, because it was meant that the minister of Jesus Christ should be the meeting place, as every priest must be, of creation's need and of God's grace.

The modern minister thus needs to deepen, to enrich, to spiritualize his nature by assimilating the best in the thought and practice of the Christian mystics. In its highest form, here is genius of a certain kind. "The saints are our masters in the spiritual life. They have the same kind of authority in their own sphere that the great poets and musicians have in theirs. We sit at their feet and learn from them what we are able to assimilate." [16] Not many of us will be able to follow the speculative side of mysticism—its philosophical aspects. But most of us can benefit enormously from a careful study

[16] W. R. Inge, *Religion and Life*, pp. 3-8.

of mysticism as a rule and a discipline of life. We will not allow ourselves to be disturbed by the visions and the rhapsodies of the mystics. For one thing, are not these also to be found in the spiritual experience of Bible characters as well? For another thing, these never bulk very large in the experience of any of the mystics, and are never sought as ends in themselves. But beyond all this, when we survey our own matter-of-fact and vision-less lives, we will ask ourselves, if love had done its per-fect work in us, if our holiness had been what it might have been, what it ought to have been, would there not be moments in our lives when we too might have said, "I have seen the Lord"? Neither will we let ourselves be turned aside by the asceticism of the mystics. Theirs was not a living death, as Dean Inge has remarked; it was always a dying life. In its extreme forms it may seem to have something repellent about it. But when I read that the German mystic Suso, after sixteen years of effort, succeeded in subduing his refractory body it makes me wonder how far the failure to subdue and con-trol our bodies may have prevented us from a fuller knowledge of God. As one reads the lives of the mystics one discovers that the hours spent by them in contempla-tion are not so much time deducted from practical forms of activity. On the contrary, the seeming inactivity is in truth profound energy.[17] Moreover, one will never forget that the great mystics were also the great humani-tarians. Eckhard commended Martha above Mary, de-claring that it was better to feed the hungry than to see such visions even as Paul saw: *"Besser ein Lebemeister als ein tausend Lesemeister."* And Tauler wrote: "One can spin; another makes shoes, and all of these are gifts of the Holy Spirit. I tell you, if I were not a priest, I should esteem it a great gift that I could make shoes, and

[17] See Hugh Benson, *The Light Invisible*, p. 120.

would try to make them so that they would be a pattern for all."[18] "The true mystic," says Ewald, "never wilfully withdraws himself from the business of life, not even from the smallest business."[19] Again Ruysbrock, the great Flemish mystic, writes thus: "Were you rapt in ecstasy like Peter or Paul . . . and heard that some poor person was in want of a hot drink or other assistance, I should advise you to awake for a moment from your ecstasy to go to prepare the food." And Teresa of Spain says: "Our Lord asks but two things of us: love for Him and for our neighbor. I think that the most certain sign that we keep these two commandments is that we have a genuine love for others. We cannot know whether we love God although there may be strong reasons for thinking so, but there can be no doubt whether we love our neighbor or not."[20] Let one read of the work of St. Teresa in Spain, or of the work of St. Catherine of Genoa, and understand how the love of God in the lives of the saints found its perfect counterpart in the love of men. But, beyond and above all of this, there is that fulness of love, that certainty of knowledge, that hunger and thirst for God and Christ which completely controlled the lives of the mystics, that put to shame our own more empty and worldly lives.

To quote a single example where one could write chapters, take this single episode from the life of St. Catherine of Genoa, which no one of us can read without serious self-scrutiny:

And two days later, when Catherine was visiting her sister at her Convent, Limbania proposed to her, since she declared herself indisposed to go to confession (although the Feast of the Annunciation was at

[18] Quoted by W. R. Inge, in *Christian Mysticism*, p. 11.
[19] *Reflections from the Mirror of a Mystic*, p. 54.
[20] Santa Teresa, *The Interior Castle*, p. 117.

hand), at least to go and recommend herself in the
Chapel to the chaplain of the Convent, who was
indeed a saintly Religious. And, at the moment that
she was on her knees before him, her heart was pierced
by so sudden and immense a love of God, accom-
panied by so penetrating a sight of her miseries and
sins and of His goodness, that she was near falling to
the ground. And in a transport of pure and all-
purifying love, she was drawn away from the miseries
of the world; and, as it were beside herself, she kept
crying out within herself: "No more world; no more
sins!" And at that moment, she felt that, had she in
her possession a thousand worlds, she would have
cast them all away.[21]

Now, one may call this what one will. But who can
question that, if a little more of this were mixed and
mingled with our own secular and intellectualized ministry, we would ourselves be holier men; that we would
know for a surety far better than we do the love of God
that passeth knowledge; that our whole lives would be
penetrated by a deeper and finer spirit of devotion; that
we would minister far more efficaciously than we do to
the deepest and most spiritual needs of men. We need
not attempt to imitate the exact method and discipline
of the mystics, but we do need to grasp their fundamental attitude, their unfaltering conviction that communion
with God must be a fact of experience and not merely a
philosophical theory, and we must direct much more
attention to the cultivation of the spiritual life, to contemplation and to prayer than belongs ordinarily to the
program of our days.

The average Protestant minister today, who seriously
endeavors to acquire familiarity with the mystical mood
and practice, finds himself seriously handicapped and

[21] Friedrich von Hügel, *The Mystical Element of Religion*,
p. 105.

embarrassed. This thing requires time, and time is what
he most lacks. Burdened with domestic cares and the
endless demands of his parish, how is he to find the quiet
open spaces, the hours empty of all else, that are necessary for the cultivation of this temper and attitude. The
problem is a real one. Yet it can be solved, because it
has been solved. At least one can enlarge by conscious
effort and the rearrangement of one's time the areas of
meditation and of prayer. The Eastern mystics, as is
well known, devote hours out of each day to the purpose.
Sadhu Sundar Singh, the Indian Christian holy man, the
reading of whose life by Canon Streeter will reward all
who take it up, never devotes less than two hours in the
early morning to devotion.

He starts the day by reading a chapter of the Bible,
at first rapidly, but making a mental note of these
verses which seem particularly rich and suggestive.
Then he returns to these verses and lingers over them
as long as he feels that he is having fruitful thoughts
on them. Then he spends about fifteen or more min-
utes in collecting his thoughts in preparation for
prayer. Then, as he puts it, the Holy Spirit Himself
teaches him what to pray for, both in regard to himself and in regard to others. For prayer, he has no
one posture. He prays sitting, kneeling, sometimes
walking. As a Sikh, he used to prostrate himself in
prayer, but now he does not follow this practice.[2]
At table, in Oxford, someone asked him point-blank
what he thought of English Christianity and English
life. He clearly found a difficulty in expressing his
views in a way that would not seem discourteous to
his hosts, saying he had not seen enough as yet to
enable him to give an opinion, but that it seemed to
him too little was made of the aspect of religion as
peace of soul. "Spiritual things cannot be discerned

[2] B. H. Streeter, *Sadhu Sundar Singh*, pp. 79-80.

without quiet and meditation"; then, perfectly naturally, he fell into a discourse on the Peace of God and the lack of it in English life and in English religion, which none of those who heard it will soon forget.[23]

If many a minister would look into his own life he would need to admit that he himself does not make enough of the aspect of religion as "peace of soul." He needs nothing so much as to "take time to be holy." He may not be able to find three hours a day for this—which was the irreducible minimum of so practical a man as Cardinal Gibbons—but by every effort of his will he must create open spaces in his day given to nothing but the cultivation of communion with God. He must practice by hard work the methods of contemplation, of meditation, and of waiting upon God. He must learn to fold his hands upon his open Bible and to wait in silent expectation until a word of God has come to him. If the modern minister would devote a tithe of the time, which he now gives to the secular or exclusively intellectual aspects of his ministerial life to this practice of the presence of God, his whole ministry would be transformed by it. Whether it be by the "morning watch" or by a resolutely closed door at certain times of the day, these moments must be had by all who are bent on the recovery and deepening of the life of the spirit. The motto, "Ambitious to be quiet" (I Thess. iv:11), which is inscribed on Dean Vaughan's tomb in Llandall Cathedral, may well be written over the sanctuary of the inner life of every minister of Jesus Christ in our modern world.

It is not, however, only time that we lack. So unaccustomed are many teachers of religion to this daily and inward and personal experience of God, that they

[23] *Ibid.*, p. 30.

find this deliberate and cultivated communion with God so difficult that they are sometimes tempted to doubt whether it is a genuine experience at all. More and more the practical ministry tends to draw men into the world of affairs, where he is dealing with concrete facts, and to draw him away from his knees, from quiet, from habits of contemplation and communion, so that even for him who is ordained to be a prophet of the Spirit the things of the Spirit tend to become unreal. What does this mean but that we must deliberately force ourselves, our whole minds, wills, affections, intellects, toward divine things? We must clear the channels in our minds now choked up by disuse; we must form habits of spiritual communion which will become to us an inestimable joy and help. We must trust those who have tried it, when they all say the same thing.

Helps to the development of the habit of communion with God now exist in abundance. The conviction is growing that, if the church is to be a great spiritual power, it will be not only through a multitude of new organizations and restless activities, but through prayer and meditation and much silent waiting in the presence of God. Thus and only thus, men have come to feel, can our whole life be lifted up to a higher plane of spirituality, of power, and of influence. Hence the growing practice of "retreats" for ministers, to which they gather for days of devotion and prayer. Hence, also, a growing literature in practical methods for increasing the capacity and deepening the habits of personal communion and of silent waiting upon God.[24]

[24] The books by Cyril Hepher called *The Fellowship of Silence* and *The Fruits of Silence* are already well known to American readers. They may well be read and pondered by all who are to be the spiritual guides and leaders in our modern world. They contain an inspiring account of an experiment in silent worship, an experiment which has been tried with success in our American churches; and directions as to the mode and method of such

Ministers today will do well to acquaint themselves with this literature. They will do well also to educate their congregations in the reality of this silent waiting upon God. Save and except the Quakers, there exists in our churches a very terror of silence.

We have yielded inch by inch to encroaching choristers and extemporizing organists, till now should silence intervene but for the briefest space, our people look up alarmed, convinced that the silence spells break-down. . . . Silence is not a gap to be filled. It is the greatest of all preparations and the climax of all adoration. As the American poet Whittier wrote:

> Heart answers heart in one desire,
> The blending lines of prayer aspire;
> "Where in My name meet two or three,"
> Our Lord hath said, "I there will be."
> So sometimes comes to soul and sense
> The feeling which is evidence
> That very near about us lies
> The realm of spiritual mysteries.
> The sphere of the supernal powers
> Impinges on this world of ours.

services are not the least valuable part of these books. They contain also practical hints to the individual who desires to develop his own powers of concentration and of communion with God. Equally valuable for such purposes is Canon Streeter's book on Sundar Singh, already referred to, which can be studied with profit by all who are in earnest in their desire to know the mystical way. Dean Inge's latest little book, *Personal Religion and the Life of Devotion*, will reward careful and reverent reading. So will Evelyn Underhill's *The Life of the Spirit and the Life of Today*. *The Mystical Element in Religion* by Baron von Hügel has just been republished in two volumes, and contains much valuable material. One will read the lives of John Woolman and George Fox, *Studies in Mystical Religion* by Rufus H. Jones, and Dean Inge's *Christian Mysticism*. Recent books are Edith Talbot's *Lessons in Meditation* and the book called *Spirit* by E. P. S. H., with a foreword by Richard C. Cabot. And there are the two little books by A. H. McNeile, also well known to American readers, called *Self-Training in Meditation* and *Self-Training in Prayer*.

The low and dark horizon lifts,
To light the scenic terror shifts;
The breath of a diviner air
Blows down the answer of a prayer:
That all our sorrow, pain and doubt
A great compassion clasps about,
And law and goodness, love and force
Are wedded fast beyond divorce.
Then duty leaves to love its task,
The beggar Self forgets to ask;
With smile of trust and folded hands,
The passive soul in waiting stands
To feel, as flowers the sun and dew,
The one true Life its own renew.[25]

As I approach the end of these lectures, however, I confess, for myself, a certain homesickness. I want to get back home before I close. I have read and I have studied and I have practiced as well as I am able the rules and the disciplines of the mystics. And I have had my reward. I have learned. I have been humbled. I have felt how much there is beyond my own poor powers of attainment in these giants of the spiritual life. Yet always I have had a certain sense of strangeness. I have not felt myself wholly at ease or at home in these rules and disciplines, these stages purgative and contemplative and unitive, these waitings and silences. And I know what I have missed. I have missed Jesus. From a Christian point of view, it is a defect of much Christian mysticism that it has made too little of Christ. Except in the case of the English mystics, the effort too often has been to make the direct ascent of the soul to God without the mediation of Christ. A similar defect will be found in many of the modern mystical writers and in their rules and disciplines. But for the Christian this can never suffice. This can never satisfy. The only

[25] Cyril Hepher, *Fellowship of Silence*, Preface.

thing that can make him happy is the knowledge of God
that comes in and through the knowledge of Jesus.[26] It
is the God in Christ which alone will satisfy the heart
of the Christian. It is the mysticism of the New Testament that I want, and not mysticism apart from it. I
want mysticism, but I want it saturated in the language
that is dear to me, consecrated by the Christ that is near
to me, made familiar and sweet by the thoughts and speech
that from my babyhood have been the spiritual home
and household in which I have lived. There is mysticism aplenty there. I find it in my Gospels when I read
that the Kingdom of Heaven is within, and that except
as a little child one cannot hope to enter the Kingdom
of God. Every branch of mysticism, according to Baron
von Hügel himself, is to be found in the later writings
of the New Testament—the experimental in John, and
the speculative in Paul. Paul, as we all know, was intimate with the methods and even with the vocabulary
of the Greek mystics, reference to which can be found
in nearly everyone of his epistles. He is the greatest of
the Christian mystics. And behind every chapter of the
New Testament is the certainty of the mystic's first-hand
knowledge of God, the authentic message of one who has
seen and known God. No mystics in all history ever
had an experience of God that can equal, much less trans-
cend, the knowledge of Him vouchsafed to John and the
author of the Hebrews. But Jesus is in the midst of it;
Jesus is the source of it; Jesus is the cause of it. The
life hidden with Christ in God is the essence of it. And
it is the mysticism of the New Testament that my soul

[26] "The living Christ comes to us as living presence and power
when the historical reality of this earthly life confronts us, chal-
lenges our attention, constrains our confidence and submission.
This is the test of any mysticism or piety; it is Christian only if
morally and religiously consistent with the truth and grace of
the historical Jesus" (A. E. Garvie, *The Christian Certainty amid
the Modern Perplexity*, p. 223).

craves. What is the Christian experience of God? I open the book of Acts and in its third chapter I read of a man lying infirm and helpless at the gate of the Temple. And I read of Peter and John coming upon him with their whole souls filled with the life and strength of God which is theirs because they have known the power of Christ's Resurrection and the power of the Holy Spirit. And I find them giving that life to the man who was infirm so that "he leaping up stood and walked, walking and leaping and praising God." And when Peter was asked how these things came to pass, he said that the name of the Prince of Life had made this man strong. That was two thousand years ago. And the Christian experience has remained unaltered. A description of it was recently given by Bishop Talbot of Pretoria, and it reads like a paraphrase from the chapter in Acts:

> When we were without hope, smashed, broken, we were again set upon our feet into a living hope by the resurrection of Jesus from the dead. Jesus had spoken of the Father loving us with a love that seeks until it finds, the love that will never let us go, not even if we crucified the Son. That is the Gospel.[27]

For myself, it is this which I want to believe with all my heart and soul. It is this Christian knowledge of God, this peculiar New Testament secret, these wonderful words of life that more than all else I want to cherish, and keep and make my own.

Thus I propose to keep close to my Bible. Above all else I propose to try to know by prayer and meditation the very heart of my Bible. We shall never have a real, new, revealed Christianity unless we understand the Bible through and through. No amount of institutional

[27] *Religion and Life*, "Christ," pp. 70, 71.

Christianity will suffice. No amount of extra-Biblical mysticism will suffice. No amount of strenuosity or of anything of that sort will suffice, unless it is rooted, gripped inside, by the primal experience of the men who were with Jesus. That is the Gospel.[28]

It goes, or it ought to go, without saying that the modern minister will be a student. By this is not meant that he will make any display of erudition, or that his sermons will be filled with pedantic literary references and quotations. But he must have a knowledge of "the best that has been said and thought in the world." He must betray his thorough training in those secular disciplines which form the background of men's thinking today. He must show his familiarity with "the geography of man's mind," and have "an easy citizenship in the different centuries which have told the tale of the human adventure." In a word, he must be a man of genuine and of growing erudition. All continuously helpful preachers have been students—hard, patient, unending readers of poetry, of history, of biography; above all, perhaps, of biography. Nothing will do a minister so much good as the reading of the lives of the great-hearts of history. A great saint of God is more worthy of our study and admiration and imitation and love than any other. Nothing in life is so ennobling, so enriching, as to know intimately and to love devotedly a truly great and a truly noble man. All of this reading will enrich the mind of the minister and provide him with a background of culture which is indispensable to all who speak to the mind of our modern world.

But, above all, the man who truly ministers to our modern world must have the mind of Christ. The object of all Christian preaching is to release by the spoken word into the lives of men the life of God which the

[28] See Bishop Talbot, *in loco,* pp. 70, 71.

Lord Jesus Christ came to bring to man. This is the preacher's specialty. All else is means to this one supreme end. Though he possess all else and do all else, but does not produce in other lives, because he does not possess it in his own, the Christian experience of God, he fails in his appointed mission.

That experience is enshrined in the Bible. For the Christian preacher to know his Bible can ultimately mean only one thing: it can only mean to know the experience of God which the Bible contains and describes. What is occasional with other men will be continual with him. A minister today will be wise who understands that the modern mind is not looking to him for guidance on all kinds of subjects each of which requires to be dealt with by a specialist if it is to be treated authoritatively. There is too much amateur talk in pulpits about questions of science and philosophy and social questions. One sympathizes with the man who left his church because he was wearied with all this and wanted an authentic message from God from a man who had had an authentic experience of God. What the modern man does expect, and has a right to expect, is that the preacher be a specialist in the Bible. And by specialism in the Bible is not meant specialism in the linguistic, literary, archeological, historical, scientific, and philosophical questions which have to do with the Bible. By specialism in the Bible is meant specialism in the spirituality of the Bible. By specialism in the Bible is meant specialism in the experience of God in the Bible. It is his specialty to show to the modern mind that the writers of the Old Testament were men of like passion as ourselves, undergoing in their own time the same experiences as ours; men who, through their genius for religion, the ardor of their piety, their sincerity of heart, their purity of life, were enabled to see the God who all the time was seeking to make Him-

self known to them.   He should show that with the advent
of Jesus came a revelation of the life of God which literally re-made human life, and re-made human society.
It is well that the preacher be versed in critical studies,
that he know all that he can of the processes by which
the books of the Bible came into existence.   But alas
for him if that is as far as his knowledge goes!   All such
studies are rather intellectual exercises than essential to
the exposition of the eternally valid spiritual teaching
and the application of the moral and spiritual dynamic
of the Bible.   It were better for the preacher to our
modern world to know the Bible thoroughly, as the
preachers of earlier generations knew it whose inspiration lay in their deep and intimate familiarity with its
message, and in the richness of their spiritual life due
to constant feeding on the Bible, than that he should be
the foremost of critical scholars.   In one of her letters,
Julia Ward Howe describes how the Bible came home to
her:

> Read James's book on "The Varieties of Religious
> Experience."   I received a painful impression of
> doubt.   A God who should be only my better self, or
> an impersonal and pervading influence,—these were
> suggestions which left me very lonely and forlorn.
> Today, as I thought it over, the God of Abraham, of
> Isaac, of Jacob, seemed to come back to me.   I said,
> Let me be steeped in the devotion of the Psalms, and
> of Paul's Epistles.   I took up the Sermon on the
> Mount, and the Lord's Prayer.   How simple, how
> beautiful, how positive.[29]

There are multitudes of people in our modern world
who are "lonely and forlorn," who have the same "pain-
ful impression of doubt."   Let a preacher out of the

[29] Laura E. Richards & Maud Howe Elliott, *Life of Julia Ward
Howe*, Vol. II, p. 315.

reality of his own experience unfold and interpret for them the reality of the Bible experience of God and he will be the spiritual prophet for whom they wait. Simplicity, beauty, certainty—these are the marks of the faith which the minister of God who keeps close to Him in that revelation, which has come to us in Jesus Christ His Son offers to our modern world.

The Christian minister will thus seek above all else the cultivation of the Christian experience of God. Nothing can take its place. It underlies his entire ministry. Alone the knowledge of God in Christ will give to his preaching that note of certainty for which men listen, for which they long. It alone will enable him to possess the knowledge of Christian truth, and to interpret aright its great and underlying doctrines. Only as he himself is daily refined and made Christ-like by his fellowship with God and with Christ will he be able to be a good shepherd of the sheep and to perform his great mission of comforter. It is out of the realities of such an experience that he will be able at the moment of common prayer to lead his people into the presence of the Eternal. The impoverishment of the Christian experience means death to the ministry and the impotence of the church. Its possession in increasing joy and sense of power means for any minister of Jesus Christ a life of inward blessedness and of untold helpfulness. The success of any ministry is in exact proportion to the possession, by him who seeks to minister in the name of Christ, of the Christian experience of God. "O Timothy, that good thing which was committed unto thee, keep through the Holy Ghost which dwelleth in us."